Stage Solos

Stage Solos

The Desert Queen * Waiting for Vern * Dickens In America

James DeVita

Three Full-length One-Person Plays

Words, Words, Words

WORDS, WORDS, WORDS PUBLISHING
608-220-5077 * jamesdevita@gmail.com

SPECIAL NOTE
Anyone receiving permission to produce a play contained in STAGE SOLOS is required to give the Author credit on all programs distributed in connection with performances of the play, and in all instances in which the title of the Play appears, as follows:

The Desert Queen
Adapted for the stage by James DeVita
with the permission of Rosemary O'Brien, author, *Gertrude Bell, The Arabian Diaries, 1913 – 1914, and* the Robinson Library at the University of Newcastle upon Tyne, UK.

Dickens in America
An evening with Charles Dickens.
Adapted from his works and words by James DeVita

Waiting for Vern
by James Devita

STAGE SOLOS

Paperback ISBN: 9781736651247

First Printing 2021
WORDS, WORDS, WORDS Publishing.
Printed in the United States of America
www.jamesdevita.com

CONTENTS

1 The Desert Queen 1

2 Waiting for Vern 41

3 Dickens in America 91

1

The Desert Queen

With the permission of Rosemary O'Brien, author, *Gertrude Bell, The Arabian Diaries, 1913 – 1914.* Also with permission of the Robinson Library at the University of Newcastle upon Tyne, UK. Original © 2006 James DeVita. Freely adapted from the works and words of Gertrude Lowthian Bell.

The play opens on the eve of Miss Bell's death. She has returned to an archaeological dig only to find it has been completely ransacked by desert thieves. She alone is left to pick up the pieces. As she sifts through the rubble of the desert and the stunning archaeological finds which have been demolished, she recalls the beauty that Mesopotamia (Iraq) once was and the unfortunate occurrences which have brought it to its current state of ruin.

ACT ONE

July, 1926, the desert, west of Baghdad, Iraq.

The ransacked site of an archaeological dig.

Upstage center a canvas tent, the front flap open, the bedding and contents obviously rifled through. Downstage of that center, a small table and two collapsible chairs. The table is on its side as is one of the chairs. Assorted shards of broken pottery and tools litter the area: small architectural stones, brushes, a broken alabaster vase, broken wooden crates with pieces of destroyed pottery still in them, journals, books and papers. A larger crate center right as a sittable.

Gertrude Bell enters. She is in her traveling clothes, hat and sand-scarf. She carries a small trunk. An indomitable, positive spirit; exhausted and invigorated at the same time. She is inured by custom to the hardships of desert life, both its climate and politics. She stops and calls off behind her.

GERTRUDE BELL

Assaf! Asaaf, wein rayeh? Aljml, min fadlik, aljml! *(Assaf, where are you going? The camels, please, the camels!)*

SHE STOPS FOR A BEAT AS SHE TAKES IN THE RANSACKED CAMP. THEN CONTINUES ON, SURVEYING THE AREA BRIEFLY.

In order properly to appreciate *dust* one must travel across the desert by camel. Eighty degrees when I started out before dawn, one hundred and ten by two o'clock. It is difficult to regulate one's apparel to a thermometer which behaves in this fashion. *(Sets down her trunk.)* This time of year, the greater part of the region is dried up and barren, barely enough herbage for the camels; a few determined tufts of grass pushing their way through the stones and sun-split mud. *(Takes out a handkerchief.)* Exceedingly featureless terrain here. A lifetime crossing it with little to take a bearing on but my camel's ears, which are not a good line.

(Takes up trunk again and crosses to chair.) One of the great difficulties is that no one knows the distances between things even approximately, and there is no map worth a farthing. *(Sets trunk down.)* An undulating, flint-covered country, until the plain has its way—and then it as though one were looking out over the level floor of the world. Silent beyond belief. No clatter of civic life, no cry of the wild, no creak of wheels. The noiseless slow footfall of camel is all the traffic you shall find here. I wonder at times why I take pleasure in such a landscape. In spite of its desolation and emptiness, it is quite beautiful. Or perhaps it is beautiful because of its emptiness. To

wake in a desert dawn is like waking in the heart of an opal.

Assaf brought me word. *(Opening the trunk.)* News travels quickly in the desert. The sentries I left here, fearing a raid from the west, abandoned the site. It turned out to be merely looters, who—as you can see—have once again destroyed more than they have taken. *(Crossing to a examine a crate.)* Distressing, yes, but not surprising. Man has plundered man here for more than five thousand years, why should today be any different. Rare is the archaeological site which has not been looted. Pillaging is a way of life here; one might almost say it is a form of commerce. *(She takes off her backpack and retrieves a canteen of water.)* We were a party of six when we started from the museum. Assaf alone has stayed on with me. Excuse me. *(Drinks.)* The others left two days ago, fearing the road too much, and returned to Baghdad. It was better so. I don't want unwilling men with me. It appears, however, that I had no need of their help. Little remains to be brought back. Some of this may be salvaged, restored—*(of a shard she picks up)*—Ubadian ceramic 5000 BC. Restoration, technically, is not always a difficult task, however iconic objects are always complicated. You needn't worry; desert thieves seldom return once they have taken what they believe to be of worth, nevertheless, Assaf—my rafiq, my guide—will keep watch.

We are safe for now, insha-allah. Others will come in their place, however, to this land where murder is, as a new-made widow once told me, "like the drinking of milk here." *(Taking off her hat and wiping her forehead as she speaks.)* The road to Baghdad has been traveled many times before. *(As she sets her hat down.)* I thought at first you might have been a raiding party—a ghazzus—a rather large one. I am relieved to see you are not. Ghazzus are not for artifacts, but will steal everything else—or worse—if they come upon you. It is a means of survival here. Since neither the desert nor the government is terribly forthcoming, steal what you can, when you can. A sort of desert industry based on a profound misconception of the laws of supply and demand.

(Examining a piece of shattered pottery as she speaks.) Yesterday we paused after sighting a thing lying on the desert with an ominous flutter of great wings over it. Assaf observed that it was three dead camels and two dead men—ghazzu met ghazzu, said he. *(Crossing to trunk again, she stops.)*

Camels will sit down and absolutely refuse to move when they are worn out. That's just what they do. I envy them their good sense.

(She rights the overturned table.) By and large these ghazzu raids are conducted without any bloodshed at all. Indeed, there are even rules which govern them. More often than not, a sort of obligatory submission occurs: outnumbered by horsemen or arms,

the weaker tribe simply hands everything over. The slighted party then, having lost all his worldly goods, bides his time, for months, years perhaps, until opportunity ripens, and then he and his tribe ride forth on their *own* raiding party and recapture everything again—and more besides—and the dispute enters on another phase. Unless, of course, a life is lost—then a blood-feud ensues. Which may last a thousand years. *(Small beat as she picks up a few shards of pottery and rights an overturned chair.)* A man's fortunes here are as varied as those of the gambler on the stock exchange: one day he is the richest man in the land, and next morning he may not have a single camel to his name. The desert dweller lives in a constant state of war. But we are safe—khair insha-allah. Still, keep a weather-eye for the casual thieves, who if they find us watchful will turn out to be fine guests, and if they find us sleeping, will lift our camels.

(Crossing to some shattered stone work.) Happily the vast majority of looters enjoy a rather elevated level of ignorance. Very primitive understanding of the concept of 'worth;' often stealing that which is of least value. *(Picking up a particular stone.)* Sadly, though, they are all too careless in their mindless pillagings. Of little interest to them is an appreciation of the world's common ancestry. Indeed, between these two rivers, they tread upon vestiges of the very birth of modern civilization.

(Closes her hands around the stone.) Imagine a great temple cut out of solid rock, the charming facade supported on great Corinthian columns, soaring upwards, and carved with figures almost as fresh as when the chisel left them, *(showing the stone)* all this in rose red rock, with the sun just touching it and making it look almost transparent. Passing through, a gorge widens, and on either side, the towering cliffs are cut out into rock tombs of every shape. The gorge continues, widening still, into a kind of square with a rude cut theatre in it, a great open place, an ancient amphitheater . . . like a fairy tale city, all pink and wonderful. A rose red country half as old as Time. *(Opens her hands again.)*

That is what these thieves cannot see. *(Crossing to one of the nearby wooden crates and putting the stone into it.)* Do not care to. Out of this crumble of carved stone, like the genie wrung from the magician's ring, rise remnants of the first wonders of mankind, *(takes up the crate and carries it over to the table)* advances in art and literature and science so great that they are nearly incomprehensible. Here, quite literally, from nothing, everything began. *(Places crate on table.)* I love the beginnings of things. I do, most thoroughly. And unless one does, I don't believe one can truly appreciate the ends of things. *(Of one of the artifacts in the crate.)* Sumerian. Third millennium BC.

(Artifact in hand.) Al Jumhūrīyah al-'Iraqia. Baghdad. Built by the Abbasid caliph al-Mansur, 762, Hulagu, grandson of Genghis Khan, sacked the city in 1258. Tamerlane, the Turkic conqueror, sacked it in 1401. It was brought under Persian control in 1508. 1534 it was captured by the Ottoman Empire and held for nearly four centuries until our British forces captured Baghdad in 1917. A country of continual beginnings one might say. *(Places artifact back in crate and taking notes.)*

Did you know there are sharks in the Tigris river? I swam it once. The current is very strong in Ba'qubah and Al Kut. *(As she speaks, she takes the occasional note on the remnants of artifacts in the crate.)* However barren this desert may seem, one seldom travels more than a mile without reaching a spot that has some intriguing name attached to it. "Nahr el 'Awaj, Nejha, Tulul es Safa, Kal'at el Beida, Ghadir el gharz." In listening to Arab talk you are struck by this abundant nomenclature. A rise in the ground, a large stone, a remnant of ruin—not to speak of every possible hollow in which there may be water—all are named, and, to the Arab, not a map needed to find them. A Bedouin guiding me across the Syrian in 1905, drew rein mid-desert, pointed to a few fire-blackened stones and said, "That was my hearth. Here I camped five years ago." The desert has a long memory. *(Small beat.)* Indeed, there is a word for it . . . which escapes me now—a word in Arabic for the *mark* left on the desert, the traces which people leave behind. Before encampments are raised, you see, rocks—*basma*, that's the word. *Basma,* a place cleared of stones leaving a sort of outline in the sand. An impression. Which can last for centuries. *(Slight pause.)*

Blue is the color for sorrow here, from the violets which bow their heads as a wind passes over them. Mourners bow their heads, clad like violets in blue robes of woe.

(Returns to taking a note in the journal.) It pleases me greatly to be here. I've spent so many months wandering the white-washed halls of the museum: arranging, cataloguing, labeling, requisitioning—I want to feel savage and independent again, which I do, in my empty desert of delights. And delights unbounded there are. I have seen the brave little geranium still flowering in the low ground; the marigold no less courageous, and it is difficult to conceive anything more exquisite than the little scarlet tulip growing upon a barren hillside; I have seen companies of them shinning like jewels among the dust and stones. The rains will come again; the clover and thistle will thrive; trees will green; and white and yellow daisies will star the stone-sprinkled landscape once again. Until then, however, there is a great deal of work to be done to set things right. Certainly we cannot leave this place in a state of disorder which we ourselves have helped to create.

What happens to one's hair in this climate? It just evaporates. Truly, it's thinning. I never was so sunburnt in my life. I'm a rich red brown. Not at all becoming. *(Spying a shard of pottery and crossing to it.)* I failed to mention that on occasion, looters, whether conscious of it or not—most often *not*—do make off with objects of great value. "The ass wears a collar of gold," as the poet says. *(She takes the piece with her and searches the area to see if any other pieces of it are to be found.)* The vase this belongs to stands nearly three feet tall, and it is—the vase is—quite incalculable in value, worth all the rest: carved some 5,000 years ago in the ancient kingdom of Sumer; upon it, the raised figure of the goddess Inanna interacting with the people of earth—quite extraordinary a detail. *(Stops her searching.)* It is one of the earliest known narratives of man. Human beings were discovering for the first time how to record a story. Writing, a relatively new idea, was being birthed; much like a preposterous baby camel, all legs and neck and nothing else; ungainly, but alive. It would take another 4500 years for our sweet Prince of Denmark to return from Wittenberg, but herein lie his very first steps. The oldest poem ever attributed to a specific author, the *Hymn to Inanna*, was discovered in Sumer, written by the daughter of King Sargon I.

Like a dragon,
you poisoned the land–
When you roared at the earth

In your thunder,
Nothing green could live.
You rained fire on the heads of men.

2300 BC.
They blamed their gods back then too.

(Crossing to the trunk, she takes a cloth napkin out of it and wraps the piece of vase in it.) The vase still may be found. I've hunted down many a priceless piece of antiquity in the back-street bazaar stalls of Baghdad, perhaps I shall find it there. Being used as a container for camel crops no doubt *(Regarding the piece of vase.)* I've always been interested in the past more than the present; the east more than the west. *(Puts the piece the trunk.)* It was Mopsa's fault. It all started with her. *(Taking a bundle from the trunk.)* My letters. I wrote this when I was six.

(Reading.) "My dear Florence, Mopsa has been very naughty this morning." Florence was my stepmother. Mama died at three. Mopsa was an exceptionally large grey Persian cat. *"She has been scampering all over the dining-room. I had a great chase all over the hall to catch her. During breakfast she hissed at Kitty Scott. I gave Mopsa your message and she sends her love. I forgot to say Kitty Scott was very frightened. Your affectionate little friend, GERTRUDE BELL."*

Where did Persian cats come from? Persia, obviously, but I was six and wanted to know more, wanted to know what this *Persia* was. It sounded magical to me. At eleven I was reading world history before breakfast, devouring every book I could find, and keeping journals—very imposing looking quarto volumes bound in leather. *(Crossing to sit in the chair, she reads another letter.)*

"Febuary 10. 1879." I was ten. *(She sits.) "Read Green's History. Lessons went off rather lazily. Went into the gardin. Looked at flowers. Breakfast. Read all the morning. Read all the afternoon. Tea. Mother read to us. Went to bed tired, had a little talk not fun and went to sleep. Woke. Read in liberry this morning."*

Liberry. L-I-B-E-R-R-Y. I never entirely mastered the art of spelling. It does *sound* like liberry, though, doesn't it? Who says li*br*ary? Or Fe*bru*ary. Irritating. Why these words merit the burden of yet another superfluous letter 'r' is quite beyond me. To this day there are words which continually confound me: 'seized" for example: i-e, e-i? 'Privilege:' there should be a 'dee' there at the end, as in *knowledge*, no? For heaven's sake, I was the first woman to take a first in History at Oxford at a time when women were forbidden to *use* lib*rar*ies; I speak Arab, German, Latin, French and Italian; I was a part of the Mesopotamia Expeditionary Force in Basrah and Baghdad working intelligence; 1920 I became Oriental Secretary to the British High Commission in Iraq; Winston Churchill himself summoned me and thirty-nine men to help determine the future of Mesopotamia; I founded the National Museum in Baghdad, became their Director of Antiquities, and was largely responsible for putting the first king of Iraq on his very throne—but can I spell 'exorbitant.' Shouldn't there be an 'h' in there somewhere? Utter torture. *(Searching for another letter.)* Actually that's a lie; not torture at all, I put very little attention on it.

"BASRAH, March 10th, 1917." I would have been forty-eight. *"We are now hourly awaiting the news of the fall of Baghdad. It's the first big success of the war, and I think it is going to have remarkable consequences. We shall, I trust, make Baghdad a great centre of Arab civilization. I received a letter from Sir Percy Cox to-day, from the Front, full of exultation and confidance."*

There again, 'confidence': 'ance'. Quite hopeless, I'm afraid. *(Pause.)* "Question the wandering winds and all that thou shalt know, from dusk until the dawn, is that they blow."

(Rising and crossing to the trunk to put the letters back.) In spite of my orthographical deficiencies, I continue to chronicle, to document whenever I can. An Arab friend once told me after I intimated I was to write a book about my travels, "When your Excellency writes a book, you will not say 'Here there is a beautiful church and the great ruins of a castle.'

People will see that through your photographs. But you shall say: 'In this village there is no water, in this one, there are no hens, and here, there are no men.' Then they will know from the beginning what sort of story it is." Perhaps that's why I'm here. Perhaps I should just do what I know to do. What I've always done.

BACK AT HER JOURNAL, SHE TAKES THE OCCASIONAL NOTE AGAIN AS SHE EXAMINES A FEW OF THE SHARDS IN THE CRATE, WIPING HER NECK AND CHEST AGAIN.

The act of writing, the actual driving of the pen—as opposed to spelling—has always seemed to me no more an effort than remembering. The desert, for me . . . I think of it almost as one vast 'remembering.' A sort of collective attic of mankind's memory, to push the metaphor, where, in a delicious rummaging, one discovers a tantalizingly dust-covered *liberry*. Its books are all about us. Orpheus with his lute could not have charmed the rocks to speak more clearly. *(Crossing down with a particular shard.)* Within the wind-worn scratches of this broken bit of mud lie the secrets of the ages, tales of daily life, lessons from those who came before us, cries forward, one might say, to the children to be, to *us*; or to the stars, perhaps; an affirmation etched in stone simply to say: I was here. I existed. I have something to say.

Surely a sentiment shared.

I have an uneasy feeling all the time of trying to take a hand in things which are too big to be guided. They move on inevitably, rough hew them how we will.

"Stick to rocks," I was once told. I have encountered worse advice.

(Returning to the table and finishing a last note in the journal.) The oldest communities of people here date back some 7000 years B.C. These shards of pottery, fashioned by some caring hands four, five thousand years B.C., are of vital import in understanding the people here, who came before. *(The crate finished, she carries it UL and places it down.)* However more civilized we hold ourselves, we did originate here, all of us, Mopsa included, in this, the *fertile crescent*—if one recalls their history lessons—the Tigris, the Euphrates, windingly chalked across the blackboards of our childhood; those magical rivers crawling through the world's 'cradle of civilization.'

The first recorded laws ever found for the humane conduct of human beings were conceived in this very place—Mesopotamia—Greek for "*between the rivers.*" Etched into a block of black basalt. The Code of Hammurabi. King of Babylon. 18th century BC. Discovered 1902, Sūsa, Iraq, formerly ancient Elam. I have a mind for names and dates. You may have noticed. *(We can see that, at times, as here, she is feeling the heat despite her attempts not to show it. She crosses to where she had placed her back pack)* Forgive me, please; I've become obsessed with details lately. They whirl about my thoughts like so many dervishes until I rid myself of them. In *my* desert, I've discovered, even the river of oblivion has dried up, for I've yet to walk her Lethe banks.

I ride camels in my dreams.

(She retrieves a bottle of salt pills from the backpack and takes one.) "The gate of God" it means: *Babylon*. One of the Seven Wonders of the World, of course. I can still see it in the picture book renderings of my school days, its hanging gardens, built, as legend has it, by Nebuchadnezzar II, 600 BC, for his wife Amyitis. Because she was homesick. Quite the gift-giver, he. *(Determined to return to working, she starts towards another crate.)* East of the Euphrates, near Baghdad, Babylon lay, utterly dazzling in its splendor. At her time, the largest and most important city in the known world; the location today marked by a scattering of toppled ruins. *(Stops. Beat.)*

"The powers of the world endure for but an hour, naught shall remain of their majesty." Hafez. Persian poet. 14th century. "Be not too sure of your crown," he wrote, "you who thought virtue easy and reparation yours. You who skip so lightly from the monastery to the wine-tavern doors."

Shams od-Din Mohammed Hafez Shirazi. *(Finishing her cross to the crate.)* Occupies the same place in the minds of Persians as that filled by Shakespeare in the minds of Englishmen. *(Picking up the crate and bringing it to the table)* The finest place in the world is the back of a good camel, and the best of companions is a good book. *(Stopping at the table.)* "Open my grave when I am dead, and thou shalt see a cloud of smoke rising out from it; then shalt thou know the fire still burns in my dead heart—yea, it has set my very winding-sheet alight." Extraordinary. *(She goes to her trunk for another pencil, taking up a light shoulder wrap in her hand in the process.)* Not Shakespeare himself has found a more passionate image for love than that. *(She quotes another Hafez verse.)* "If the scent of your hair were to blow across my dust when I had been dead an hundred years, my moldering bones would rise and come dancing out of the tomb." *(Beat.)*

It's the first hours of night which I find the worst. *(She shakes out the shoulder wrap which is still in her hands.)* How I manage to collect so many fleas among so few possessions is an insoluble mystery to me. *(She crosses up to the tent and drapes the wrap over a portion of it.)* There's hardly a suitable place for them to lodge in. They must show a great deal of skill and agility beyond the common wont of fleas in order to get themselves packed up and carried off each time, but that they are equal to the task I can attest. *(Crossing back to the trunk to take out what-*

ever else might have fleas on it.) I often wake in the desert with an uneasy sense of having fallen asleep on an anthill. *(At trunk, takes out a tin.)* My little bit of heaven: khawah, the bitter black coffee of the Arabs, better than any nectar; passed from hand to hand within clusterings of black tents with a 'deign to accept' and returned with murmurings of, 'May you live.' *(Takes out her tea dress. Shaking it out, she stops for a moment and holds it up to herself.)*

One must do their best to endure the discomforts of travel in style. Yes, we come to the sordid but serious question of clothes. I confess, in Basrah once, I had sent me a lovely blue shot silk gown with a little coat and its own hat trimmed with feathers, a purple satin day gown with a cape, and a mauve parasol. I believe the inhabitants found me just as exotic as I they—*more*, perhaps. *(Crossing up, she drapes the dress on the tent.)*

Basrah. So utterly beautiful when I first came upon it, wonderfully cool and delicious. *(Crossing back to the trunk.)* But the floods were out, and the banks of the Euphrates were under water. The Ark and all the rest become quite comprehensible when one sees Mesopotamia in flood time. *(Takes out a pair of shoes.)* On the way to dinner one evening with my friend, Mr. Lawrence—"of Arabia" I hear he is called now—very fitting—I emerged in a pair of overly-large rubber boots beneath my silken gown and was forced to tread paths more like steeplechases than walkways, continuously interrupted by irrigation channels, over some of which you leap, while over others you do a sort of tightrope dancing across a single palm trunk. I shall fall in certainly, I thought, and either be disgustingly muddied or drowned, and then Mr. Churchill, who was waiting for us, and dear Lawrence, would most assuredly have the laugh of me. *(The lightness of her tone during this speech changes slightly.)* To spite them both, however—and many others—I did not drown. *(Starting up toward tent.)* They laughed at my appearance nonetheless. *(Tosses the shoes into the tent and crosses back down to the trunk, attempting to cover a growing frustration.)* Things were always greatly enlivened when Mr. Lawrence was present. Endless talks were had and vast schemes devised for the government of the universe, since not one of us could agree on the government at hand—

PAUSE.

I believe we should wait for the sun to lower. It is too hot to make any sense of all this at present. *(Calling off.)* Assaf, jib alshai, min fadlik. Jib alshai. *("Assaf, the tea please.")* I will pause for tea and then continue.

(She sits.) 115 degrees is the limit of human endurance. The moment the temperature rises above it, heat stroke begins, and when it drops below, it ends. It reduces my mind at times to a state of mad-

dening feebleness. It's no good ignoring it—one has to knock under till it cools, confound it.

We could have saved many lives if there had been any cool place to put the men in.

(Pause. She waits for Assaf to bring tea.) I have invented a scheme which I practice on the worst nights. I drop a sheet in water and lay it in a pile along my bed between me and the wind. I put one end over my feet and draw the other end over my head and leave the rest a few inches from my body, producing a little wall of cool air between me and the world. *(Looks upstage to see where Assaf is. Looks back to the audience and smiles.)* Excuse me. *(Rises and crosses up, calling off.)* Assaf? Jib alshai, min fadlik. *(Retrieving her tea dress and wrap from off the tent ropes.)*

Assaf possesses a remarkable ability to sleep during the hottest parts of the day. Rather nocturnal sort of fellow. Makes very good tea, though—oh, and the nights here; night brings with it such a great procession of stars gaining the sky: Sirius sparkling out; the Great Bear; the sickle of Leo; the Twins, and Capella's lovely face half veiled in heat haze; Aldebaran following after, forever in chase of the Pleiades, all as clearly visible as when the ancient Babylonian astronomers first wondered at them, when the Milky Way appeared so bright that its light actually cast shadows upon the ground. A marvel barely visible at all from any large city today where on a cloudless night one will see less than one percent of what the ancients could see.

The stars have not become dimmer; rather, the earth has become brighter. But not here. Here it is still as dark as it has ever been. *(Pause.)*

Excuse me. I will rest a moment, insha-allah. And change for tea. Maasalaamah. Fi aman illah. Fi aman illah. *("Go in the safety of God.")*

SHE ENTERS HER TENT,
CLOSING THE FLAP BEHIND HER.

End of Act One

ACT TWO

During the intermission, tea has been set.

Ms. Bell enters from the tent dressed for tea, a light shoulder wrap also on her. She has recovered and looks refreshed, but as the act progresses, one can tell it takes a greater and greater amount of energy for her to ignore the heat and to rise above a deep sense of weariness and frustration. But she continues to rise above them both, determined to work or to engage in the questions which begin to perplex her more and more.

She looks out at the audience for a moment.

GERTRUDE BELL

I fear at times you may all be merely a mirage. You shimmer before me. You see, it's difficult at times to see straight or even to think straight when temperatures run this high; things often don't fall into scale. One gets bewildered, and, believe me, there are enough materials here for bewilderment. *(Starts toward tea.)* Perhaps it is I that am the mirage. Although I must say I feel anything but shimmery this evening; the moment I stop moving I drip ceaselessly. I might wander Acheron an hundred years and never cool. I hope heaven is chilly.

(Sits to tea.) Everything you touch here is hot: a book, a spoon, all the inanimate objects, your hair—if that's inanimate—the biscuit you eat, the clothes you put on. One longs for the river, to lie on its banks, to wash, to bathe. Although it is very difficult to make a curtsey with grace when you're wet in a bathing dress. To whomever one might meet.

(Starts for tea. Stops.) Delicious word, *mirage*. From the Latin *mirare*, 'to wonder at', a derivative of *miraculum* . . . miracle. *(Pours tea.)*

The rain may come at any time. You never know when. This is a country of extremes. It's either dying of thirst or it's dying of being drowned. Crossing the Nefud desert once, a great storm marched across the path in front of us. Lightning flickered through the cloud mass, the thunder spoke from it, and on the outskirts companied of hail, scourged and bent by a wind we could not feel, it darkened the world quite suddenly. Yes, they come. The rains. More often than one might imagine. "Like Niobe, all tears."

Shakespeare. My constant companion, he and Hafez.

This storm I spoke of, came upon us torrentially, blotting out the path before us, and bringing with it thunder and rain so heavy that silvering pools soon stood twinkling in the thirsty sand. I rode on, head bent into the wind, till Assaf' yelled that we should lose our way, there being no landmarks to be seen. I was forced to agree and we quickly made up camp. I sat in my tent and read *Hamlet* from beginning to end. As I read, the world swung back into focus. Princes and powers stepped down into their true place and there rose up above them the human soul conscious and answerable to itself. When the storm had passed, just before sunset, I stepped out of the tent—oh, but the wet sand smelled good. I stood on the top of a hill and saw wings of rain sweeping away from us, leaving the land sunbathed. Assaf led the way again, his cotton clothes clinging to his drenched body, and gave thanks for the rain. "Please God, it goes all over the world."

(Takes a sip of tea. Short pause.) Not a very cooling occupation, tea. *(Of the tea.)* This is about the last thing left of my former existence. To those bred under an elaborate social order, such as myself, rife with custom and ritual, few such moments of exhilaration can come as that which stands at the threshold of wild travel. The gates of the enclosed garden are thrown open, the chains at the entrance of the sanctuary are lowered, with a wary glance right and left you step forth into a life of adventure and enterprise. Into it you must go alone, separated from the troops of friends who walk rose gardens, roofless, defenseless, without possessions. You leave your sheltered life, and, like the man in the fairy story, you feel the bands break that were riveted about your

heart, and there before you . . . the immeasurable world. I am a *person* in this country. *(Short pause.)*

Do you know what I look forward to very much? A leg of mutton. That's not very poetic, is it, but you should see the meat on which I've lived. I can't even think what part of an animal it grows on. I've lived almost my entire adult life on tinned milk, tinned meat, and tinned butter. I have grown extremely tired of tinned things. I have forgotten what a potato tastes like. *(Smacks a mosquito.)* In proportion to its size, this area must have the largest number of mosquitoes of any inhabited spot on the globe. *(She rises and takes off her shoulder wrap.)* They goad one to distraction.

(She gently folds the wrap and places it in the trunk, and pauses.) I have been the guest of kings. I have made kings. I have sat in gardens after dinner with Baghdad lanterns hanging in the trees, beside walls sheeted with scarlet-red roses, such as I'd never seen—the very night blushed with them—and I thought myself in a half acre cut out of Paradise. *(Beat.)* My mind wanders in this heat. *(Crossing to the canteen.)* The trouble with wandering is it has no end.

(She wets her handkerchief and cools herself with it.) It's amazing, though, to be brought face to face with millennia of human effort and then to consider what a mess we've made of it. It is almost impossible to believe that a few years ago the human race was

more or less governed by reason, and considered consequences before it did things. Fortune, it seems, did not intend kings to be wise. Our soldiers go down before you can wink, before their number's dry. *(Beat.)*

It will not cool. There's too much to be done. *(Crosses back to table.)* We can't just sit here. *(Puts tea set up onto the tray. Stops.)*

At times I think we did a certain amount of good here—*are* doing good. I don't mean to mitigate our oversights . . . many issues should have been resolved before the occupation, but there was no one to do it, no one who had ever thought of it. *(Retrieves one of the crates and a cataloging book and brings them back to the table to continue her work.)* And it was left to our people here—not in London—the soldiers and officers *here*, in the field, to thrash it out, in the face of growing resistance and in the middle of a war. No one really knows exactly what they want here, least of all the Iraqis, except that they don't want us. *(Beat.)* I wrote about it. I wrote it, I know I did. *(Goes to the books strewn about in front of the tent. Rummaging through them, she finds her journal.)* I am as guilty as anyone—I've never denied that—of oversights, of being swayed by passions. *(Crossing to DR sittable crate.)* But we were in the middle of a full-blown jihad. It was no longer a question of reason, we had to *do* something. *(She sits, looking through the journal.)* What a dreadful world of broken friendships have we created. We rushed into this business with our usual disregard for a comprehensive political scheme. *(Knowing the date.)* January 22, 1921. Yes. Yes, here it is. I was sure I did.

"Britain imposed the idea of a united Iraq but it was never wholly accepted. The Arab government, which is predominantly Sunni, does nothing to conciliate the Shiites, who are in the large majority."

July 14th. *(Searching for the next passage.)* Yes. I wrote again.

"There's no getting out of the conclusion that we have made an immense failure here. The underlying truth is that we promised an Arab Government with British Advisers, and we have set up a British Government with Arab Advisers." *(Retrieving a letter from her journal.)* And here, Sir Percy writes: "The public at home now is thoroughly disturbed with the turn things are taking here and a strong agitation is at work demanding that we cut our losses and evacuate the country." *(Beat.)* Yet we are pledged here. We have an immense responsibility to these people. But when we try to hand power over to the Arab Government so that we can leave, the extremists delay us in doing so, which means they must be made to submit to force, but the Arab Government *has* no force till its army is organized, therefore it cannot *exist* unless we lend it British troops, and therefore we cannot leave. We're like the daughters of Danaus, condemned for eternity to pour water into a pitcher which has holes in it.

The end of the Roman Empire is a very close historical parallel. *(Rises and drops her journal on the sittable crate. Crosses back to the table to continue her work.)* Many of these circumstances could not have been foreseen, yes, but still that doesn't excuse us for having been blind. How can England, who has managed her own affairs so badly, claim to teach others to manage theirs better. And the response to my concerns: "Gertrude Bell is a silly chattering windbag of a conceited, gushing, man-woman, globe-trotting, rump-wagging, blethering ass!"

PAUSE.

I have much less control over my own emotions than I used to have. The quality most needed when dealing with these situations is not, as some have wrongly stated, courage, but *patience*. My fairy godmothers neglected to endow me with it. Perhaps I shall learn how to practice it before I leave here. If I have not, it will not be for want of opportunity.

SHE STEPS OUT FROM BEHIND THE TABLE.
PAUSE.

It's so . . . frighteningly complex.

You see, we wanted so badly to bring in Mosul and Basrah, and the tribal sheiks, many of whom had had never even seen Baghdad. *A united Iraq*. You must understand, there never was anything quite like it before. The idea was amazing! The bringing together of an essentially nomadic people—it was literally the making of a new world! March 11, 1917, Baghdad fell. Six days later the British force arrived and General Maude spoke to the city.

"People of Baghdad, in the name of the King of England, and in the name of the people over whom he rules, our military operations have as their objective the defeat of the enemy only! Our armies have not come into your cities and lands as conquerors, or as enemies, but as liberators! It is our wish that you should prosper even as in the past, when your lands were fertile, when your ancestors gave the world literature, science and art and Baghdad was one of the wonders of the world."

There was such promise! Endless celebrations. There was a great Boy Scout function held. There were 1500 Iraqi Scouts and Scout Masters. All the balconies were crowded with people and the great open square too. There were some 5000 spectators. Besides the ordinary Scout exercises, which they did extremely well, they took the opportunity of introducing a little nationalist propaganda. They made the newly created Iraq flag in *living boys*, dressed in the national colors, and they drew in chalk over the square a huge map of the united Iraq, with the borders formed by a *line of boys*—and each of them with Iraq flags indicating the three towns, Basrah, Baghdad and Mosul—with the crowd crying out: "Three cheers for King Faisal the First!" It was all so wonderfully moving. I turned to an Arab friend in the middle of it, and embraced him, and assured him that complete independence is what we ultimately wished to give. "My lady," he said, "complete independence is never given; it is always taken." *(Long pause.)*

The road to Baghdad has been traveled many times before. It is too full of the memories of ghosts, joyful ghosts, jaunting about on camels before the world cracked and foundered. I don't like the look of those ghosts—they are too confident.

Doom'd for a certain term to walk the night,
And for the day confined to fast in fires,
Till the foul crimes done in my days of nature
Are burnt and purged away.

As the poet said.

It will not cool. *(Beat.)* Anaximander, a Greek philosopher in the 6th century BC, postulated that all things eventually return to the element from which they originated. I find myself here. I feel, actually, *inside* the desert. As if I've become a part of it. And at last, I am beginning to see more clearly. It's as if finally a thing shows itself to you and you know you're glimpsing an understanding of something you've struggled with all your life, and a perspective on humankind at last looms within grasp . . . and there's no one to tell it to. *(Beat.)*

I have to leave here now.

Yes. I feel it's time for me to leave.

(Calling off.) Assaf, besora'a! Msaadh li! Yajebu an athhaba al aan! Msaadh li! *(Assaf, hurry! Help me! I have to go! Help me!)*

SHE BEGINS TO GATHER UP A FEW OF HER BELONGING AND PUTTING THEM IN THE TRUNK: HER RIDING CLOTHES WHICH ARE IN THE TENT, HER JOURNAL AND CATALOGUING BOOK, ETC.

Gather up what remains, *again*. Restore what we can, *again*. Oh, but it's a great game we're playing here, and some day we shall have much to say about the general principles of it—and of the players. Leave them to heaven. *(Shuts the trunk lid.)* Although I must say the Almighty has shown Himself decidedly neutral in this affair. *(She picks up the trunk, but she is too weak to lift it now. She drops it back onto the chair.)* Assaf, besora'a; msaadh li! *(Assaf, hurry, help me!)*

SITS STANDS STRAIGHTENS HERSELF UP. A MOMENT.

Camels will sit down and absolutely refuse to move when they are worn out. That's just what they do. *(Crosses and sits down. A long pause. She takes in the audience, then the sky.)*

Have I told you what the Tigris is like on a hot summer night? I shall not be able to form even the remotest conception of how marvelously beautiful it is. At dusk the mist hangs in long white bands over the water; the twilight fades and the lights of the town shine out on either bank, with the river, dark and smooth and full of mysterious reflections, like a road of triumph through the mist. Silently a boat with a winking headlight slips down the stream, then a company of smaller skiffs, each with his tiny lamp, loaded to the brim with watermelons. "Slowly, slowly," the voices call across the water. "Don't ruffle the river lest we sink—see how we're loaded." And the larger vessel slows that the wash may not disturb them. The water is so still that you can see the constellations in it, star by star. The waves of the passage don't even extinguish the floating votive candles, each burning on its own minute boat, made out of swathes of a date clusters, which anxious hands launched from somewhere above the town. If they reach the last town—yet burning—it is believed, the sick man will recover, the mother shall find her son, the baby will be born safely, and all shall be well in this world of hot darkness and glittering lights and bewildering reflections. Khair Insha-allah.

(Pause.) I have to leave here now.

SHE RISES AND CROSSES TO THE TABLE. SHE PICKS UP THE ROSE RED ROCK WHICH IS IN THE CRATE, AND TAKES IT WITH HER. SHE GRABS HER HAT ON THE WAY OUT, STOPS AND TURNS TO THE AUDIENCE.

As-salaam alaykum wa barakatuhu, fi amman illah. Fi amman illah. *(Peace be upon you and blessings. Go in the safety of God.)*

SHE PUTS HER HAT ON AND EXITS.

The End

FIRST PRODUCTION

The Desert Queen was first produced by American Players Theater in 2006, directed by James DeVita. Gertrude Bell was played by Sarah Day; costume design was by Holly Payne; sound design, Rory Harkin; scenic design, Harland Ferstl; and the stage manager was Evelyn Matten.

NOTES

I had spent quite a bit of time searching, rather unsuccessfully, for a female historical figure about whom I could write play. I was reading short encyclopedia bios on literary figures, artists, female explorers, and quite a few queens, but nothing really caught my imagination. I needed a hook, a subject who would excite me enough to want to spend the next year or two of my life researching and writing about them. A friend of mine, and director, James Bohnen, suggested the name Gertrude Bell. I had never heard of Ms. Bell, but on my first search of her name I found a picture of her in the desert, elegantly dressed, perched on a camel in front of the Sphinx. To her left, on a camel also, was Winston Churchill, and to her right was T. E. Lawrence, or Lawrence of Arabia as we've come to know him. I read on a little further and saw that she was referred to as the Desert Queen and, immediately, I wanted to know more about this woman. That was the hook I'd been looking for, the desire to know more of someone.

Born into a wealthy family on July 14, 1868, Gertrude Lowthian Bell attended Oxford University at a time when women were still being set apart in classes; they were forbidden to use the libraries or receive degrees, and in one class, Gertrude was even forced to sit with her back to the professor. In spite of these handicaps, she took a First in Modern History in 1888, the first woman in the history of Oxford University ever to do so.

She traveled extensively as a young woman, making two trips around the world, pausing only to climb the Alps. In 1892 she made her first trip to the Middle East. "She fell in love with the desert and its archaeology, and between 1900 and 1913 journeyed over 20,000 miles, from Istanbul to the Syrian desert, from Damascus to the Tigris." She taught herself Arabic and led her own caravans. A lone, unveiled woman in a male Muslim world, she traveled deep into the Arabian desert, and despite the danger, met with continually warring tribal chieftains, learning their ways and those of the desert. She drew maps and supervised archaeological digs, documenting everything as she went: "the feuds and alliances, the routes and water sources, the flowers and the ruins." When World War I broke out, Miss Bell's knowledge of the desert routes and tribal alliances suddenly became valuable military intelligence. In 1915 she was given the rank of Major Miss Bell, the first woman officer in the history of military intelligence. In 1921 Winston Churchill summoned the greatest experts on the Middle East to a conference in Egypt to determine the future of Mesopotamia and to create the country of Modern-day Iraq. The conference included 39 men and Gertrude Bell.

"She was an acknowledged archeologist, a courageous traveler who dined with china and crystal, dressed in extravagant clothes, rode on a camel and horse, and was the most powerful woman in the British Empire in the years after WWI. She was named to the high post of

Oriental Secretary and achieved nothing less than a miracle by creating the modern state of Iraq."

She was also a prolific photographer and took over 7000 photographs between 1900-1918. Those of Middle Eastern archaeological sites are of great value because they record structures that have since been damaged or in some cases disappeared altogether. Between 1923 and 1926 she founded an archaeological museum in Baghdad and became Iraq's honorary Director of Antiquities

She died of an overdose of sleeping pills on the night of July 12, 1926 at her home in Baghdad.

WAITING FOR VERN

2

Waiting for Vern

ACT ONE

A BARE STAGE BUT FOR TWO CHAIRS.

A SCRIPT ON EACH.

LIGHTS UP.

AN UNCOMFORTABLY LONG PAUSE.

THE ACTOR ENTERS

THE ACTOR

I'm here! I'm here! I just got--God, I am so sorry. I can't believe I'm late. I can't believe it. I--this is perfect. Of all nights--I--this is just perfect. I apologize. Thank you for--I was in, I got um . . . traffic. Traffic around here is just--I mean, between the construction and, and then the parking--I couldn't even--it's blocks! Blocks away I had to--I'm sorry. I am so sorry. I know, I know, don't say you're sorry just don't do it again, yes, I know that, that's what I say myself, so--heed my own, of course-- but I am sorry. I apologize. I'm sorry, but I need to say that . . . so that's out there. Thank you. Thank you.

Okay. I' here.

HE GOES TO HIS CHAIR, CONTINUING TO TALK AS HE'S SETTLING IN. HE PICKS UP HIS SCRIPT AND SITS.

Okay. Just a second. I just got to--there we go, there it is, just like they said, it's right--I just got to--okay.

You wouldn't believe this day.

A MOMENT. HE NOTICES HE IS ALONE.

Excuse me a sec.

HE LEAVES THE STAGE. AFTER A SEARCH, HE RETURNS.

Um, um . . . we seem to have a slight problem here folks. Uh . . . this is incredible, but, um, I don't think Vern's here yet, and, uh, he's the other character, actor, plays the other character, and um, I don't think he's here yet. *(Looking at watch.)* He should be here any minute, though. I'm sure he'll be here in just a minute, so if you'd just um . . . he'll be here in a minute.

HE SITS. A LONG SILENCE.

I think the traffic got him. It does that. Traffic. Indiscriminately. At random. *(Pause)* I really do apologize for being late. It's not like me at all. I'm never late. Never. Really. Ask anyone. *(Pause)* I'm usually early. 'Better an hour early than a minute late.' That's what I say. That's my motto. In life that's my motto. Lateness. I hate it. Makes me crazy. So I understand how you must um . . .

This isn't good. This is not good. I can't believe this. Really, again, I apologize about the delay. I'm sorry Vern's late. I'm sorry for everything. He'll be here. I know he will. He does this all the time. He's always late. *(Pause. He points at the empty chair.)* This is very unprofessional. Very. *(Pause)* And you are all being just wonderful about this. And if you'll just bear with us a little bit more, I'm sure he'll show up and we can get on with the evening. And the reading. So please have patience. *(Pause.)* Thank you.

PAUSE. NOTICES THAT THERE ARE ONLY TWO CHAIRS.

Nice set.

I don't function well under these circumstances, I don't. I'm sorry. I would try to get things moving here, start a conversation or something, pass the time a little, but I'm not good at this, that, I'm not good at spontaneous . . . talking. I'm not spontaneous like that, I'm an actor. I get to say other people's words and then I don't have to think about what I'm saying or . . . what I say, or . . .

I'm not prepared for this. To be honest with you, and I'm going to be very honest with you here, I'm a little self-conscious right now and not a little tense. I have tension. It's a thing I get. At times. Particularly while I'm waiting for something. For something to happen. For someone to show up. Waiting for a show to show up. *(Pause.)* When he gets here we'll just start over. From the top. I promise, we'll go from the top--DO-OVER! Do-over. So until then maybe we could just pass the time a little 'till he shows and then go on from the beginning. Okay? *(Pause.)*

There's quite a few of you here. More than I expected. More than they told me to expect. I was under the impression there would be, um, there would be just a few, not many, people here to listen to this, this new script, and, just a few, like--but I guess not. I was mistaken. I was misinformed. Or rather ill-informed as to what to expect. Here. I see that. I assumed. I know, I know, never assume, never assume, yes,

I know that now, so--*(of the audience)*--but this is good. This is like a bonus. I'm sure that what they told me was just in case only a few people showed up. You know? Which is a smart thing. I can understand that. Too. 'Don't expect anything and you'll never be disappointed.' That's what I say myself. I understand. So welcome to this. All of you.

SILENCE. LOOKS AT WATCH.

Guess that minute's up, huh? Well, I didn't mean minute like 'minute', like actual time. Just like a sort of 'he'll be here in a little bit' kind of a minute. A subjective minute.

SILENCE.

Traffic got him. That's what I think. Traffic. 'Cause if I know Vern, and I know him, he was probably in the left lane, and you know what that means. Vern is a left lane kinda guy. Me? Right lane all the way. Never miss an exit. Right lane, I can get off any time I want. Left lane, in traffic? You just get sucked along with it, out of control. Probably where he is. *(Pause)* 'Right lane,' that's my motto. Stay to the right and you won't be late. A rule I live by 'cause, *(gestures to the empty chair)* 'cause this is what happens! The traffic gets you and then it's just all over. 'Cause once it gets you, this traffic thing?

It's like being inside this huge animal that you get stuck in the middle of but it doesn't have a head or a tail, just a middle, everywhere is the middle, you're just in the middle all the time! Where's the front?! That's what I'd like to know. Where's the front of traffic? And, and, who's first? It could be anyone. Like, okay, like if I was in traffic right now and I was a car and there was a car in front of me, okay, this car in front of me could be like, let's say, the fourth car in this thing of traffic, which would make me fifth, right? Or, or it could be like five hundred and eighty-nine or something, which would make me--so I could be any number, couldn't I? It could even be, this car in front of me could even be the last car in this thing of traffic, which would make me first! *(Pause)* I could be in the lead and not even know it. And who wants that. *(Pause)* Stay to the right. Don't be late.

SILENCE

This is great, isn't it? This is just great. It's perfect. I should have known. I never learn. I never know when to say know. I am a wimp that way. I said I'd do it. This. This script here. 'Coupla quick bucks, just a cold reading, two characters, no rehearsal, so I figure what the hell, I can pull it off, I'm a professional. And to be honest with you, and once again, I'm just going to be very honest with you tonight, I don't even know what it's about. The script. I haven't had a chance to read it the way this day has been. Not that I didn't try. I did. I tried to get the script before coming over here. To work on it. To prepare. I really did. I'm a very responsible person. Very professional, but--ask anyone--but of course, somebody had already sent the script over here, to the theater, where I wasn't. Anybody tell me? No. Great. So there I am, you know, rush hour, now I gotta try and fight my way over here, to the theater, which of course, was on the other side of where I was, to get a look at the script. The day has not gone well. I mean, I planned ahead. I always do. I thought all this out. I figured I would get the script around four-forty-five or so and then I would work on it until the traffic went away and then I would come on over here and work on it right up until curtain, but, you know, the best laid plans . . . when it comes to traffic. It just got me. Him too, probably, that's prob--*(he hears a noise offstage)* Did you--? I think he's here. Just a second. I think he--*(he runs off the stage. Peeks back in another entrance.)* Did he--? Okay, just a sec, I think he's---*(leaving again.)*

SILENCE. HE ENTERS AGAIN.

Nothing. *(Pause. Looks at watch.)* He's really late. Like quite a bit already. *(Pause.)* So what do we do now? What to do. We wait. *(Pause.)*

I guess we should do something. In the meantime. While waiting. Something, um . . . I could tell you a little something about myself but that's probably not a very good idea so I won't do that.

We could, um . . . we could maybe introduce ourselves to each other, you know, we could get the house lights turned up and then we could all take turns and--or, or! I could um, no, no, that's no good, bad idea . . . *(eyeing the script)* . . . we could, um, I could . . . *(goes to pick up script, then doesn't)* . . . we could wait a little while longer. It hasn't really been that long. Just feels that way.

Like when you're in traffic.

Which is probably where he is, was, Vern, but I'm sure he's out of it and he'll be here any--*(starts to leave the stage)*--I could just! I should just! *(Doesn't leave.)* No, no, I'm sorry, I'll wait, I'm being hasty, I--this is just unexpected. And that's okay. I can adapt. I said I'd do it. I gave my word. And I'm here. For now. I'm a professional.

HE EYES THE SCRIPT AGAIN.

We could, um . . . we could, I mean, I could maybe . . . read the play. Out loud, of course, to you. I could read both parts maybe, and then when Vern comes, very shortly, we could just start over from the beginning. We could do that. And maybe while I'm reading we could at times pause and . . . discuss parts of the play or something. We could have a dialogue with each other. You could participate in this with me. Okay? Okay.

GOES TO READ THE SCRIPT BUT STOPS.

Um, now one thing, before I start, if I am to do this, to read this script which I'm not prepared for, alone, I just want to say something. That this is a cold reading. So I've never seen this before and--I'm not trying to apologize for anything up here, I'm just trying to give you the facts, that I haven't had any time to prepare anything for--well, that's not exactly true, I got a description of my character over the phone and--I wrote it down. I have it here. I'll show it to you. Usually with me the kind of descriptions I get are like, 'Five foot whatever, anxiety issues . . . twenty-five to thirty.' Or a simple, 'Ethnic thug.' *(*Please feel free to fill in appropriate description of the actor playing the part.)* Not this time, though. OK, here we go. This is what they give me. I'll read it to you. *(Reading.)* "It's you. Just be you." *(Pause.)* That's great isn't it? That's, that's just wonderful. Full of insight, huh? I mean that's it. I swear to God that's all they give me. I'll show it to you. *(Showing it to audience.)* Okay? So that's all I'm out here with. Just so you know. No apologies up here, just facts. *(Returning to prepare to read script.)* I'm just trying to be responsible. OK. So, we go.

GOES TO READ THE SCRIPT BUT STOPS.

Maybe I should tell you a little something about the kind of characters I tend to play when they ask me to just be me. I think that they think that I'm like that. But I'm not. Not at all. It's just something I do, and it gets me jobs so I let them think what they like, 'Just do what you do, don't be creative!' I here that all the time. So anyway, the kind of character that I tend to play in a play is usually a case. His mind the, the way it works, is not normal. He has thoughts about extremely weird things, as I tend to. Things that can't even be thought. I'll give you an example . . . I use this all the time, to prepare . . . it's like trying to think yourself to the end of the image . . . of a man painting a picture of himself painting a picture of himself painting a picture of himself painting a picture of . . . yes? You know what I mean?

Could you imagine if you thought thoughts like that all the time? If they hounded your every idle moment? Well, that's me--him, the character I tend to play--always getting himself into situations where these thoughts arise. They are attracted to him.

Give you another example. I just got to--(he searches through his things)--just one sec here, I need a, I just got, I . . . could I borrow a pen from someone? Does anybody have a pen? I'll get it right back to you. I promise.

THE ACTOR KEEPS ASKING UNTIL HE GETS A PEN FROM AN AUDIENCE MEMBER.

Thank you. Hey. A PROP! Something! *(Pause.)* Where was I? Oh yeah, the pen. I was going to give you an example of how my character's mind works. That I would play. OK. Here we go. What do you see here? You probably see a pen. An ordinary pen. A . . . *(actor should describe whatever kind of pen he receives each night)* . . . 'Micro FaberCastell-Uni Ball' plastic . . . kind of capped pen. You see that. I look at this pen, me, the character, I look at it and before you know it I'm wrestling with the mysteries of the Universe. How does this work, you might be thinking? I will tell you.

HE CAREFULLY PLACES THE PEN SOMEWHERE ON THE STAGE.

Here we go. Okay, so, I look at this pen, I see a pen, okay, and my mind begins to hum a little bit. . . it kind of clicks in and then, well, we're off. It begins something simple, like this:

Okay, if this is a pen . . . where did the pen come from? So there's a pen, I see a pen, oaky, probably some guys *made* the pen. Some guys in a factory somewhere put a bunch of parts together and made this pen. So okay, my mind goes, my mind goes:

Then where did the *parts* come from to *make* the pen? Okay, so, I can handle that, okay, so there's like this . . . other factory somewhere, where these guys make these parts that they send to the guys who put the parts together to make a pen. So I'm alright so far, you know, my mind is okay, it's just being kind of curious right now, kind of playful, but I can sense the pace picking up a bit. It continues:

Then where did the stuff come from to make the parts? Okay. Okay. So there's like these, there's . . . it's got to come from some kind of plastic, right? Which is made out of minerals or something, stuff in the earth--

Then how did the stuff get in the earth?!

Now it starts to get interesting. Okay, so the stuff had to get in the earth from somewhere, so naturally the next question is where did the earth come from and now I'm in to planets and stars and things. And they're all supposed to come from some . . . mess in the beginning, so I think myself all the way back to that, and then I'm there, I'm in the mess, and I try to think back more, further than that, to what was before that, before the mess, and when I do what I come up with is this kinda really tiny white dot surrounded by black. *(Pause.)*

I mean I've thought this frigging pen back a billion years, and the problem is, where my mind gets a little crazy, is not being able to think past that tiny white dot. I get stuck. Right after the mess. I can't think one more thought past the dot. I can't make it disappear. 'Cause, 'cause if I could, if I could make the dot disappear then there would be nothing left but the black that surrounded it right? BUT, but . . . you can't have just black 'cause if there's no Universe or nothing then how could you have black 'cause there can only be black if there is something for there to be black in! *(Pause.)*

I am alone in these thoughts. I am myself alone. And then what happens is, if you let these thoughts take control, they eventually skip all the middle stuff and you start going right from pen to dot. Shoe--dot! Chair--DOT! Audience--LOTSA DOTS! Okay? This is my trial, my cross in life. I am in combat with these thoughts all the time. This army of little white DOTS, pulling me, sucking me in. It sometimes takes every ounce of energy I have to just stay where I am. To keep my mind here. 'Cause when I go away, the only way I can get out of there, the only way I can come home, is to kind of distract myself, to put my attention on something else, something outside of me, something . . . out there. . . . out THERE! *(Pause.)* It's a constant battle to do this. *(Gesturing to his head.)* It's very busy in here. Very busy and very scary. Yeah, you don't want to be in here.

PAUSE. COLLECTS HIMSELF A BIT.

Well, that would be my kind of character in a nutshell. *(Pause.)* It's like math. Hurts me just to think of it.

SILENCE. RETURNS THE PEN. SILENCE.

Passed the time a little.

SILENCE.

The play. Right. I was going to read the play that I'm not prepared for because I was late. *(Going back to script and preparing to read it.)* OK. I'll read and . . . well, I'll just read and we'll see what happens. We'll be spontaneous together. Unless somebody would like to come up and keep me company?

PAUSE. HE GOES TO READ THE SCRIPT. DOESN'T.

You know, maybe that wasn't such a bad idea I had. Maybe we could get the house lights turned up and we can all take turns and introduce ourselves to each other. Good idea? Okay. *(Talking to the light booth.)* Excuse me! *(To audience.)* Excuse me. *(To booth.)* Excuse me! Could we get the houselights turned up, please? *(To audience.)* Plus, Vern will probably be here by the time we each get a chance to talk so, um, yes, this is good, this is a great idea. *(To booth)* Hello! Can we have the house lights up? Hello? . . . can you hear me? *(Pause.)* Can you give me sign or something if you're up there? Could--*(to audience)*--I know there's someone up there--*(to booth)*--Hello! Could you please participate with us a little? *(Pause.)* Look, I've been very patient down here, and so has our audience, very patient . . . I don't think this is an unreasonable request . . . I--*(to audience)*--am I asking too much here? *(To booth.)* Hello! ANYBODY! *(Pause.)*

Asshole.

BLACKOUT.

Shit. *(Pause.)* Great. This is great. What the-- could . . . could you give me a break, here, please. What do you think this is some kind of joke? You think this is funny? This is not fun. This is not me having fun. Hello! Could-- *(Pause.)* Okay. I'm sorry. I'm a little on edge here. That was very unprofessional of me. I'm sorry if I offended you.

THE LIGHTS COME UP.
THE LIGHTING IS NO LONGER GENERAL.
THERE ARE ODD SHAPES AND SIZES
TO THE SPOTS OF LIGHT.
THERE ARE QUITE A FEW OF THEM.

What the hell is this? I asked for houselights!

THE LIGHT WHERE THE ACTOR IS STANDING GOES OUT. HE RUNS TO ANOTHER LIGHTED AREA.

Oh, shit. Okay, okay. I'm sorry. This is--*(this lighted area also goes black. He runs to another lighted area.)* Shit! Okay! I'll shut up. I'll shut up! This is, this is . . . *(the other two areas come back up.)* YES! Look at this. This is great. This is just great. I like this much better. Much. Yes. It's got a design to it . Design is good. Structure. I love it. Yes. This is good. *(He moves about the lighted areas.)* The, the . . . sparseness . . . it, it, it . . . represents . . . something. *(Pause. Looking about.)* You have defined the space for me. Uh, huh. Uh, huh--narrowed my choices . . . yes, yes! This is great. This, I, okay, let me see . . .

THE ACTOR STUDIES THE LIGHTS AND THE POSITIONS OF THE TWO CHAIRS. AFTER CONSIDERING WHAT TO DO, HE MOVES VERN'S CHAIR TO ANOTHER LIGHTED AREA.

There! This is wonderful. I no longer have to aimlessly wander the stage. I now have AREAS! That I can go to. *(He goes to an area. A moment.)* And leave from. *(He leaves the area and goes to another.)* I'm not waiting anymore, I'm doing. *(To booth.)* Thank you, this is great! *(The actor plays in a few of the lighted areas.)* This is almost fun! *(He goes to the spot where Vern's chair is. Then he bolts back to his chair. Pause.)* This is the story of my life, making something out of nothing. *(He stops playing.)* This is boring. *(He repeats something which he has just done.)* This is not as bad. *(He stops doing it.)* But this is boring. *(Pause. To booth.)* Are you bored up there? Of course not. How could you be bored with all this DRAMA going on down here! Beautifully LIT drama, I might add. Excuse me, um, do you have an opinion on how it's going? A little advice? Some direction? *(Pause.)* Would you like to make an announcement maybe? *(Pause.)* You're like a Sphinx. A big Sphinx. A sitting Sphinx. That's what you're like!

SILENCE.

That's what my Uncle Mikey used to call me. The Sphinx. My mother called me the Cloud of Doom. As a kid I didn't smile and I didn't talk. I thought it was a waste of time. If I did talk I mumbled. My mother yelled at me every day, 'Open your mouth when you talk!' The first time she came to see me in a show she said, 'Twenty years I haven't been able to hear you across the dinner table and now I hear every word you say in a theater with five hundred strangers. What have you been doing?!' I don't know. I guess it was all those years of bottled up sounds just coming out. I finally found words to put them into-- somebody else's, but they were still words, I was still speaking, and that's always good. Actually, it was pretty easy once I started, once I opened my mouth. This new toy I found. I was so excited. Like a kid. I read out loud all the time, newspapers, billboards, bumper stickers, whatever . . . these word things were wonderful, these things in my mouth that I'd never felt before . . . this language thing, it fascinated me. I didn't know how to use it with other human beings, but it was a start, it was a beginning on, on the road to dialogue, to . . . languaging. And I realized that it wasn't that I couldn't talk, I just didn't know how, I had never been given the opportunity, or taken it or something, I just needed to learn it. So I went to school. A speech school. I don't know, where else do you go to learn how to talk? Better. I thought at that time that there was some way to talk. Some right way. My speech teacher almost had a heart attack the first time she heard me. I was her worst nightmare. To this day I remember her face all scrunched up and furrowed when I read Shakespeare in class. Poor lady. I got rid of a Long Island accent that you could cut with a knife, though. You wouldn't know it, but I'm classically trained. *(Pause.)* I am! I can do that Shakespeare stuff.

HE WALKS INTO ONE OF THE LIGHTED AREAS. HE DOES THE SHAKESPEARE WELL. VERY NATURALLY. NOTHING AFFECTED ABOUT IT.

"What is a man if his chief good and market of his time be but to sleep and feed? A beast, no more. Sure he that gave us such large discourse gave us not that capability and God-like reason to fust in us unused."

Piece of cake. Now where I get confused, though, is which guy is me? The guy that can do that Shakespeare stuff or the guy right here.

Language is such a curious thing. It fascinates me. People make me up the way they hear me. You know? Like, when people hear me, like this guy right here, talking to you, they hear me and they think . . . he does not do Shakespeare . . . put him under . . . 'Neurotic Ethnic Thug'. You know? That's what they make up. I know they do. They look and listen once, and make up what they want, but they don't know me. They don't know anything about me. They don't know where I've been, or the things I've done, or what I believe in . . . they don't know any of that. And they're probably not interested. But I have these things. *(Pause.)*

I have no idea where this bozo is. It's all his fault, this . . . I met him once at an audition. He was late that day too. I should have known. Auditioning. Auditioning is not a natural state for a human being. It's like, I mean, you don't hire a carpenter and say, 'Could I see you carp a little something first?' Or a doctor, and say, 'Could I see you do a little something? Nothing big. Some minor surgery, local anesthetic? Just cut something up right where you are. That's it! Improvise a little!' You know!? It's not a natural state. There are very few people who could do whatever job they do, well, with six people staring at them from behind a table with pencils in their hands!

So, anyway, I met this guy Vern at an audition. A professional one. Which is a very orderly thing. There are stage managers there that are very precise in what they do, they take down your name, they give you your own little block of time, you know when it's your turn, when you're going to go. You are prepared for the event. But if one person is late, or misses their appointed time, everybody gets shifted up a slot and chaos is come. Everyone is now one time slot less prepared for their audition.

Guess who walks in late? First off, he's one of these people who love to call attention to themselves by always being late and then describing in great detail the insurmountable odds they had to overcome to make it there at all--which makes them a *hero*--which really pisses me off! So already we're in trouble here. I am not amused. And then, of course, he's a charming little shit. In two minutes he's got the whole office laughing and so GLAD that he's there! That he made it! That he--I WAS THERE! I was there! I was there all the time! I was EARLY! Nobody acknowledged that. Nobody came up to me and said, 'Oh, we're so glad you're early. You must have gone out of your way to get here before us.' No. Nothing. Piss me off.

And then he's so nice to everyone, shaking people's hands--nobody shakes hands at auditions! I want to bite his fucking hand off. And the whole time he's, of course, still breathless from his *ordeal* trying to make it there on time, playing the martyr for all it's worth, telling everybody, 'Oh, I hope I didn't keep anyone waiting.' Waiting. Waiting!? You little numb-nut, you're LATE! Late means SOMEBODY-WAS-WAITING!

Of course, I didn't say that, I *thought* to, but I didn't. So, anyway, he had arrived. We were all now back to our original time slots. Order had settled upon us. We were calm. And then he goes to the stage manager and says, 'Excuse me. I've been running a little late all day. Haven't had much time to prepare. Do you mind if I go later?' *(Pause.)* Of course, she smiles at him and says 'yes', and he smiles back, and then he comes over to me and smiles and says, 'You're next. I'll go later.' *(Pause.)*

I said, 'Excuse me?'

He goes, 'You're next. I'll go later.'

(Pause) Now I was going to give him a piece of my mind. I was. But you have to understand

that I now knew that I had even less time to prepare for my audition, so I went back to trying to memorize my script because I'm terrible at cold readings, but I can't concentrate 'cause now all I can hear in my head is this guy going, 'You're next. I'll go later. You're next. I'll go later.' So then I start to think to myself, Whoa, whoa, whoa . . . no, no, wait, wait, wait, wait--what later? What, what are you doing? What are you doing, Vern? *Vernon*. Who, what, who are you anyway?! This was a very simple thing, 'You go. I go.' But no, now we got, 'I go. You go?!' What is that!? What's going on here? This is chaos. Next time it could be "I go. I go!" Who knows? I may never go at all! There's no order left! What are you a trouble maker?! There are rules, Vern! Society has rules. It's taken hundreds of thousands of many years to arrive at this, this . . . civilization. And it only works if we're civil about it. 'I'll go later.' Oh, that's great. That's just great, coming from you . . . you who, who, who are a LATECOMER! Telling me that. Chaos, that's what we'd have if it was up to people like you. If everyone listened to Vern. CHAOS!

(Pause.) Actually, that last word came out. I didn't just think that part of it, I said it. Loudly. CHAOS! I screamed, I couldn't help it, it just came out, CHAOS!! I scared the hell out of half the room, the stage manager dropped her

coffee, and this guy Vern shushed me. He actually fucking shushed me! He doesn't even know me and he shushed me! Told me to relax. Can you think of anything more unrelaxing than somebody telling you to relax?!

So I'm thinking this guy's got a lot of nerve, I'm just about to say something to him when the stage manager stands up and says it's my turn, 'My turn?!' I said, 'My turn?!' again this guy shushes me! I'm going to kill him. Now, I'm trying to memorize my lines for the audition but I can't concentrate, 'cause now all I can hear in my head is this guy shushing me! So finally, I said to him, I did, I turned and I said, 'Don't shush me. *(Pause.)* Okay? You don't know me, so don't shush me. I may be a little tense, but I don't need to be shushed.'

'Relax,' he says. 'And don't tell me to relax! Don't. That's, that's right up there with shushing people. That's annoying. That's an annoying habit. You should be more sensitive to these things.' He's like this sensitive!! I don't know why I let the guy get to me. Story of my life, I let everything get to me! I should have said something to him right away, I should have laid into him! You know the more I think about it, I'm glad he's not here. I hope he doesn't show up! He's nothing but trouble, the little shithead!

LONG PAUSE.

Oh, god. What if something happened to him? What if he had an accident? If something dreadful happened? oh, shit. He could be hurt. I'm such a jerk. Maybe we should call his home or check the hospitals or whatever it is you're supposed to do in these situations. Maybe I should go look for him. No, no . . . I should wait. I should wait for him here where he'll know I'll be. In case he needs me I should actually be where I am.

SILENCE.

I hope nothing bad has happened. I hope he's not dead.

Then again, he could be sleeping. At home. Asleep. While I'm here waiting for him. Waiting for a sleeping person. That would piss me off. If he's not dead that is. *(Pause.)* Of course, now he'll show up and I'll be so glad that he's NOT dead, that he made it at ALL, that I'll never get to tell him what a little shithead he is!!

Damn it! I did it again. I hate when I do this. My mind, what it does. In these moments of confrontation, I, I diffuse myself. I do it all the time. My mind short circuits my mouth. It's hard to explain my mind, the way it works, there's just so much going on in there . . . at once, it's so loud! I need . . . distance from things that occur. I have limited responses to things that occur. I admit it. I either react violently to them or my mind takes a detour with the situation and doesn't come back for half a day by which time there is no situation to react to!

It's very frustrating. *(Pause.)* It's like . . . somebody cuts me off on the road? I want to get pissed off at them, but I can't! Because my mind jumps in and starts imagining that this guy is, like, on the way to the hospital where his pregnant wife is in a coma. Dying! Or he's dying. Or something like that. I know it's crazy, but my mind does that. It just makes this shit up. It's starts a conversation and finishes it without me! So I sit there stuck. I'm like a buck in headlights. And I don't know how these thoughts get in there, but they're there! Swimming around. The guy that cut me off on the road? My mind will have the argument in my head and resolve it before I get a chance to open my mouth, because of course it works out that the guy in my head *says* something like, 'Oh, my pregnant wife is in a coma, dying!' And then my mind goes, 'Oh, shit, I'm so sorry. Now I understand.'

What is that!? And after a while this all starts to happen a lot faster. Like, you remember with the dots? How you start to go right from pen to dot, skipping all the middle stuff? Same thing here. I go right from confrontation to giving them their excuse. So in the long run I short circuit myself in, like, two secon--no, not even, a second. This is quick. It happens fast.

And I wonder if this isn't a male kind of thing? Because the women that I have come into contact with in my life have never seemed to lack the ability to tell me exactly what was on their minds at any given moment. I admire this. I do. I don't always *enjoy* it. But I admire it. That freedom. That . . . immediacy. The men in my life, in my family--me, we don't do that. We're careful about things. We are wary of . . . something. We don't exactly know what it is, but we're wary of it and we expend a great deal of energy trying to avoid it.

It's whatever the thing is that will not let me sit with my back to a door in a restaurant. Anybody know this? Anybo--yes? I know. It's silly isn't it? It's like some stupid leftover from the wild west, when you didn't know who was going to come in the doors guns blazing. I know, you laugh, but that fear is still there. Somewhere a couple of excess genes that still have these thoughts on their minds are in there! I mean, it's not my fault the way I am, it's genetic. I think maybe that's what it is. I blamed everything else I could think of, it's the only choice that doesn't come back to me. I blamed God. Well, I didn't start with God, I started with my parents. Which led to God. Because, of course, I figured, if I blamed my parents, they could just as well turn around and blame their parents . . . who could then turn around and blame their parents, who could then turn around and blame their parents, who could then turn around---do you see the way this is going? You see one of those patterns emerging here? Yes, so do I--but you know me, I can't help but run with this thought and in a matter of seconds I'm face to face with Adam and Eve! Then they turn around and point their fingers at You Know Who. WHO, then, turns, none too happy mind you, and points his all-knowing finger--I see it as this HUGE finger-- back at them, they turn back around, and we're off again! Whizzing through the centuries! Pointing fingers over oceans, across continents, through cities, back to my ancestors, to my great, great, great grandfather, pointing to my grandmother coming over on the boat, pointing to my mother, pointing to my father, point his all-knowing finger at me! *(Pause.)* I'm right back where I started. So, I think it's genetic. Maybe. Could be.

LONG PAUSE.

I'm talking a lot. I know. It's keeping my mind quiet. I wish I could just shut it off but it's a mind of its own. At times.

SILENCE.

I wish he would just come. Now. *(Pause.)* Guess not. *(Pause.)* I'd be glad to know that he's okay, even though I don't particularly like him. I would.

LONG SILENCE.

'The angel of silence has passed over us.'

PAUSE. LOOKS AT WATCH.

If we were doing the play that you came to hear, this is probably where the intermission would be. But we're not.

SILENCE.

OW! Damn it. *(Pause.)* Feet hurt. Running here

PAUSE. GOES AND SITS IN HIS CHAIR AND STARTS TO TAKE OFF HIS SHOES.

Something to do. *(Looks in one shoe.)* Nothing. *(Looks in the other shoe.)* Nothing. *(Taking off his socks.)* Exciting, isn't it? Nope. *(Inspecting his foot. Pause.)* Feet are funny. Someone said that to me once, feet are funny. They are though aren't they? Look at 'em. They're funny looking things, feet. *(Pause.)* Sex. They remind me of sex. Feet do. Isn't that the strangest thing? I'm sorry, I know that sounds weird, but they do.

The first time I ever heard about sex I had no shoes on and I was staring at my feet. I was too numb to look anywhere else, and to this day every time I take my shoes off I think of sex. Isn't that weird?

My brother told me. We were in a fort. We built forts when we were kids. In the woods. Out of branches and stuff. And I had no shoe on because I thought I was an Indian. Complete cultural appropriation before there was a word for it. I went around for years without any shoes on because I wanted my feet to get calloused so I could walk on rocks and stuff and not hurt. I saw this movie, *Man in the Wilderness.* I always wanted to be a man in the wilderness, alone against nature, communing with birds and deer and all that stuff, no shoes . . . my brother told me. I don't know why this even came up at the time Maybe he felt the need to, that I was ready or something. I don't know, how old was I? Eight, maybe nine? We were sitting in this fort, in the dirt and he was trying to explain this to me using the bird and bee stuff, and when that didn't work he started to use animals, and finally he just cut to the quick and used people . . . and that's when I remember staring at my feet. And then that's when he told me that that's how I got here, that my father did this thing to my mother and you . . . you know . . . you, you get a baby . . . me. And I almost killed him. I lost it. I started screaming, swinging, I was flailing at him. 'Not my mother! My mother would never do that!' I couldn't believe it. I was so hurt. I said . . . first . . . if . . . my father would never do that to my mother and my mother would never have that done to her! It was . . . I . . . AHH! I couldn't believe it. It didn't work in my brain. I wanted to KILL him! *(Pause.)* Well, I eventually got over it, but that was a very traumatic experience for a kid, you know? To hear that. In the woods. Barefooted. Maybe if it was broken to me a little more scientifically, with colored diagrams and models, or something, I might have handled it a little better, but out there in the trees . . .

SILENCE.

I wonder why my father never talked to me about it. Well, he never talked to me about anything, really. And I never talked to him. *(Pause.)* Eternal Antagonists. Fathers and sons are. Somebody said that once too.

PAUSE. HE RISES, SHOES IN HAND. NOTICES THAT THE LIGHTS ARE NO LONGER ODD SHAPED SPOTS. HE LOOKS ABOUT FOR WHAT TO DO NEXT. GOES OVER TO VERN'S CHAIR AND PLACES THE SHOES IN FRONT OF THE CHAIR. HE STANDS BACK TO LOOK AT THEM.

I come from a family where if you don't talk about something, it never happened. *(He adjusts the shoes so that the toes are splayed apart, heels together.)* You can make lots of little unpleasant things disappear like that. Or seem to. *(He mirrors the position of the shoes with his own feet.)*

(Softly.) Ta daa . . . *(Pause.)* 'If you don't have anything good to say, SHUT UP!' That was my father's motto. We had a very quiet house.

HE STEPS OUT OF THE POSITION HIS FEET WERE IN.

I really think it's in our genes. It gets passed on. This lack of dialogue. I really it goes way back. WAY back. I think there are relatively few problems with modern man, male--ME--that can't be traced back to a couple of left-over neurotic genes. I've thought a lot about this.

Picture this . . . everybody go back a couple a billion years. You know, big birds, big animals, big everything. Now, as we know from historical finds and what not--science--the men in this age had to go out and do most of the hunting and stuff like that, you know, fighting saber-toothed tigers, dodging tar pits, mammoths, whatever, and the ladies had to, you know, stay home in the cave and watch the kids and all 'cause--no, no, wait, wait, wait, I know what you're thinking, you women you. It's not what you think. It's not that. You're going to *like* this one. It's not that the men were any better at the hunting or anything like that, it's just that the men were disposable. You know? They just didn't matter that much. There was plenty of 'em to go around. A couple a guys get killed, who cares, but you lose one of the women, first off, they can't stay home in the cave to watch the kids so the guys can go out and hunt, second, there won't *be* any kids to go hunting for! And now the whole tribe is in trouble!

You don't think some of those genes are still roaming around in us? Wondering if we're going to make it back from the hunt? Knowing somebody'll just take our place if we don't? This could be where it all started . . . these original living conditions! So I think . . . maybe . . . we're all born a little neurotic. Males. Maybe. I mean, we surely did not choose this. The guys just turned out a little harder . . . a little more cautious. 'Cause they didn't know anything about being more . . . open or whatever. Being open ain't going to help you when you're up against a mammoth. They're not interested in that. So the guys naturally developed, you know, this edge to them . . . in the woods all the time, hunting, sleeping in the rain, always looking over our shoulders and protecting things too . . . feeling responsible, and um . . . you know, we lost a lot of guys back then. And I believe that this fear, this fear of death, is still with us. It runs our lives. Every day we walk down the stree--we may not even be aware of it--but we walk down the street wary of that mammoth with our name on it! Lurking behind every corner, tusked bared, this hairy little grin, black beady eyes, just waiting, just waiting to fucking impale us! To crush . . . me.

PAUSE.

I've put some of thought into this, as you can see. And then there's more, 'cause today we want, you know, the guys to be more like the girls, and girls to be more like the guys, and to be honest with you--and again I'm going to be very honest with you--I'm a little confused. I'm a very confused person at times. Don't get me wrong, I think everybody should get out of the cave and hunt, whatever, I mean, I'm modern! I'm trying to see past the lens, which I know I see everything through. But I kind of miss the old days--even though I know now they were a lie--like in the old movies where the guys were guys, girls were girls, the good guys were good guys and the bad guys were dead. Simple. No big mystery. But today we got all kinds of stuff going on. And, I'm trying to learn, I am, but sometimes it's hard. I mean, there is something to be said for, um . . . clarity. Clarity is a very beautiful thing, I think, it's not as confusing. And don't get me wrong, I think people should be who they are, and they should be accepted for who they are, even if you don't understand them--especially, I think, if you don't understand--because how can you judge something if you don't understand it? That's what I believe! The problem is you start to get one group telling you you should be more like them, or less like you, or more like whatever--and it's, it's really confusing! I mean, you try that stuff with countries you get war! And I think, I think, maybe, people are the same way . . . they're just smaller countries. So you got to respect their, um . . . you know, their customs and things, whatever, even if you don't understand them, 'cause . . . 'cause they're just in another country. You know? And these other countries could be beautiful, we just never been there. And it's *their* country, anyway, you know? It's theirs. Maybe they don't want to go to Peru. Fine! 'Cause this messes people up. It really does. Wondering who we are, what we should be . . . what others should be . . . what country we should go to . . . who are we to, you know . . .

SILENCE.

Feet are funny.

SILENCE.

I have my father's handwriting. Isn't that amazing? If I was to run with that thought . . . I'd write like God. *(Pause.)*

I try to learn from these . . . thoughts. I try to learn from my mistakes, so I've had a lot of opportunities to . . . learn. I've read so many books and heard so many opinions that I don't know who to believe anymore. I know all the warning signs and I watch for them. Diligently. But I can't help feeling that they keep showing up because I spend so much time looking for them. Even when they're not there to begin with, they show up.

My ex-wife told me that I planned the demise of our relationship from the day we met. We were so happy I thought this has got to be temporary. I always told her this can't last. The day she left, she told me I had finally convinced her I was right. *(Pause.)*

My success in relationships since then has been upwardly . . . marginal. I mean I'm not a monk, I go out, I date. I met a woman last month. Nice woman. We went out a few times. We had dinner last week. The night was wonderful. She wasn't late, great dinner, I was even talking. I felt really good about it. We stopped at her place on the way home for a drink and, you know, nothing more than that, we're still just getting to know each other, and I felt really good! My mind was quiet, I was having fun, she asks me if I want a drink, I say 'Yes.' She he goes into the kitchen to get it and I'm out there alone, right, and she's got this huge mirror above her bookshelf, and I look in this mirror and I'm smiling. I'm smiling at myself. I'm happy. And then I happen to glance down at the books that were on the shelf. And there were--I counted them--there were twenty-seven 'How-To' books on the male- female relationship. *(Pause.)* I look back in the mirror and I'm not smiling anymore. I look toward the kitchen whence she went, then back to the books, the 'Why-Women-Love-Men-Who-Hurt-The-Women-They-Date-Who-Hurt-The-Men-They-Love' books. And suddenly the evening doesn't seem nearly as inviting as it did a moment ago. Why, I don't know. And you know me, of course I can't help but run with this new information, and I start to envision this impending interview/audition that's going to compare me to whatever criteria is in these books! ' What is she doing in there!? ' I'm thinking. And now tension has set in. I have tension. I am now waiting for her. The kitchen door opens. She returns with drinks . . . plying me with alcohol! She's smiling too . . . I'm ready for her though, I start to feign distraction. I stop talking. She gives me the drink and asks me if I'm okay. I mean, give me a break here! I just met this woman! 'Am I OK?' What does she expect me to dredge up six years of therapy because she offered me a nite-cap? Pour out my soul?! All the while I'm thinking this I'm trying to get a window open, any window, to get some air in here, I can't breathe, they're all locked! With screws! Who is this woman who screws her windows shut! Now she's not smiling anymore, yes, now she's judging me, comparing to some, some standard, to some book! 'I can't breathe in here', my body is screaming, 'I can't breathe!' So finally I said to her, I did, very politely, I said, 'Excuse me. I had a lovely evening. Thank you very much but I can't breathe.' *(Pause.)* And I went home. We never had a chance. *(Pause)* It's a vicious cycle. *(Pause.)* I mean, I don't want to make the same mistakes twice but I still want to be able to do . . . the first things . . . once. I think.

SILENCE.

I over-react. I know. I do that sometimes. This has happened before in my life. Quite a bit actually. I don't deny that a pattern has emerged. And the only common factor in this pattern, the only constant . . . is me.

I'm always there.

PAUSE.

I should talk to someone. I know. Someone who knows more about this stuff than me. But somebody who's salary doesn't get better if my life gets worse. You know what I mean? *(Pause.)* Like my father. I always wished I could have talked to my father, and I would have if we did that but we didn't, so . . .

I always wanted my father to talk to me, to ask me questions . . . real questions. He never asked me real questions. I mean we talked occasionally, you know, how you doing for money? How's work? But nothing real. Nothing of import. Even on the day I got married he didn't say anything. Nothing. *(Pause.)* I mean, at the least, I thought he would maybe shake my hand

and give that look that fathers give their sons when they get married. You know what I mean? That look? You see it in the movies all the time. The proud father standing at the head of the table, he's about to make a toast, he's kind of choked up so the words don't come . . . so he just looks at his son and then shakes his hand . . . a little harder than he ever has before . . . and a little longer . . . and they both just look at each other . . . a little harder and a little longer than they ever have before. And they now understand something, between them, between two men, that couldn't be understood before. They're now a part of something, something ancient, a sort of fellowship. And that look, you know, that handshake, is kind of like your initiation or something. And you don't get that . . . you feel like you just snuck in the back door, like nobody saw you coming in, like it was no big deal . . . but it is a big deal. We have just so many rites of passage left in this world today and, excuse me, this is a pretty big one, puberty is a piece of cake compared to this, and nobody told me I was *in*. Nobody gave me the secret handshake. Nobody looked at me differently, but I was different . . . and it would've been nice to have that kind of acknowledged, you know? Somebody could've at least said something. It's not every day a man gets married. *(Pause.)* Or divorced.

PAUSE.

I am not bitter. Disappointed, yes. Bitter, no.

(Beat.) I will ask my son all good questions. I mean, of course I care how he's doing for money and all, but I'm going to ask him, you know, about his goals and . . . ambitions and stuff. I'm going to ask him what he thinks about our president and what he . . . could he recommend a book for me to read or something. I'll talk to him about being a father and a husband and . . . I don't know . . . whatever I can think of, I'm going to talk to him about. And I'm going to make him talk to me 'cause you gotta do that sometimes with kids, and others--ME--sometimes you gotta do that, 'cause we're just . . . you just gotta sometimes. And when my son gets married, I'm going to look him straight in the eye and shake his hand harder and longer than I ever have before and I am going to welcome him in to . . . whatever this is, and let him know that he's a good man and I'm proud of him.

PAUSE.

I don't blame him, though. My father. I could. But it's not a particularly useful thing to do at this point in my life. To blame. Anyone. *(Pause.)* Even if it's true. *(Pause.)* I used to make up that it was his way of teaching me. By not talking to me. It was like a game. I pretended that he wanted me to learn things on my own. I figured I might as well make it up that way since there wasn't going to be anything there anyway, I might as well make it up useful. And I really believed it. 'Cause I think there might have been a few times when he did try to speak . . . to help, but because of what I made up in my head, I thought he was just trying to test me. To see if I'd take the easy way out and ask him for help . . . he would win if I needed him. *(Pause.)* So there we sat . . . two Sphinxes. I made it up that way.

Like a game we both wanted to win.

SILENCE.

I don't mean to be knocking my father here. We didn't have a bad relationship, we just didn't have a meaningful one. And that's a shame. Because I think we could have been helpful to each other. *(Pause.)* I mean, we had something once. When I was young. We went fishing a lot. My father took me fishing all the time when I was a kid. That's the one thing I remember we had together. Our fishing trips. I could never sleep the night before, and we'd both get up at like four o'clock in the morning and make salami sandwiches and hard-boiled eggs, and then I'd sleep in the car on the way out and on the way home we'd always stop and get slurpees at the Seven-Eleven. Watching my father eat a slurpee . . . like a kid. I mean, we had that. That's a real father-son thing. And I remember, I couldn't have been more than seven or eight, I remember being out there and not saying a word to each other for hours . . . just out there . . . fishing. And when they weren't biting . . . I would say a prayer to God to please let my father catch a fish. I would tell God that he could have all the fish I was supposed to catch that day, 'cause I just liked being out there fishing. With him. *(Pause.)* I did that. I was just a boy. But I wonder sometimes today, on those days that we both didn't catch anything, if maybe he could've been saying the same prayer too . . . and they kind of voided each other out. *(Pause.)* I don't know. *(Pause.)* I doubt it.

SILENCE. A MOMENT. HE GOES TO THE EMPTY CHAIR WITH HIS SHOES IN FRONT, PICKS THEM UP AND RETURNS TO HIS CHAIR. HE PUTS THEM BACK ON WHILE SPEAKING.

If I wasn't an actor I'd be insane. I would. It's therapy for me. If I couldn't get up here and play people who are worse off than me, I don't know what I'd do. Luckily for me most plays don't consist of well adjusted, happy people. If they did I'd be out of a job.

Of course, some plays have normal people in them, but there's always someone like me, like the characters I tend to play, and the conflict between normal and me is how we get drama. I mean, being sane and well-adjusted is just fine for everyday living, but on the stage, let's be frank, it's a little boring. Who wants to come to the theater to see a bunch of happy people!? Romeo and Juliet would be a pretty boring play if everyone, like, communicated responsibly and shared their feelings, I mean, give me a break! If anyone in that play stopped for a single second and really thought about what they were doing to each other, they would never do what they did to each other--THAT'S what's dramatic about it! They don't stop and think for a second. These are not cautious people. They're excessive people, passionate, dangerous people. "Doom eager." I read that somewhere once. These are not people who wander aimlessly around a stage waiting for something to happen, for something to occur in their lives--they make things happen! These people own their own lives and they don't apologize for them . . . they're not, they're not . . . they're not this! *(Gesturing to himself.)* They're not this.

SILENCE.

I think we should just . . . I think we've waited long enough. He's obviously not coming, so let's just . . . *(picking up his script)* . . . we still got a few minutes left, so why don't I do a quick read of the play and we can all of us go home. *(Pause.)* Then if people ask, we can at least say that we listened. We can say that we were here, tonight. That we were where we were supposed to be. And awe can say that we waited. Long enough.

HE OPENS HIS SCRIPT TO READ AND DISCOVERS THAT THE PAGES ARE BLANK. HE PUTS HIS SCRIPT DOWN AND CROSSES TO THE OTHER CHAIR TO LOOK AT THE SCRIPT WHICH HAS BEEN ON IT SINCE THE BEGINNING OF THE PLAY. AS HE CROSSES, HE SPEAKS SOFTLY.

There's nothing it.

HE PICKS UP THE SCRIPT FROM THE CHAIR AND OPENS IT. IT, TOO, IS BLANK. PAUSE.

Nothing. *(Long pause. To audience.)* Is this some kind of joke? *(Pause. Realizes it's not a joke.)* What do I do now? *(Pause.)* I could do anything I want, I guess. I could leave. I could stay. I could talk. I could not. I could do anything I want. *(Pause.)*

HE SITS, SLOWLY, IN THE CHAIR WHICH HAS REPRESENTED VERN, AND LATER, HIS FATHER.

THIS IS THE ONLY TIME IN THE PLAY THAT HE SITS IN THIS CHAIR.

I could do anything I want.

HE TAKES A SLOW GLANCE UP TO THE LIGHT BOOTH. BLACKOUT.

FIRST PRODUCTION

Waiting for Vern was first produced by the Collision Theater Ensemble in 1993, directed by C. Michael Wright. The ACTOR was played by James DeVita.

The lighting design was by Andrew Meyers.
The set design was two chairs

First published by Encore Performance Publishing 1994.

NOTES FROM THE FIRST PRODUCTION

In 1987 I saw a one-character play that was created and performed by a remarkable actor from Holland named Jozef Van Den Berg. It was called *Waited Long Enough.* In his program notes he referred to his play as a sort of tailpiece to *Waiting for Godot.* I like to refer to *Waiting for Vern* as my tailpiece to his tailpiece to *Waiting for Godot.*

DICKEN IN AMERICA

3

Dickens in America

ACT ONE

A bare stage but for Mr. Dickens' podium. A small side-shelf attached to it holds a water decanter and glass.

Mr. Dickens, carrying his script, enters. He arranges the podium and prepares to read, acknowledging the audience silently as he does. Throughout the performance he will speak directly to the audience, sometimes scripted, sometimes not. If there is applause after certain readings, he acknowledges them as is befitting, and can feel free to ad-lib appropriately. His usual style of performance has always been simply to read his selections, with very little comment in between. Not so this evening. This night is very different from all of his other nights.

It is the last performance of his career.

DICKENS

Good evening.

ABOUT TO BEGIN, HE STOPS.

I should like to take this opportunity to express my heartfelt thanks to all of you kind people for joining me here tonight. I am delighted to find myself here in the Midwest *(please fill in appropriate location – it can be more specific if desired, i.e. town, city).* I find myself often up with the sun while on the road, and the spectacle of each dawning day, suddenly unmasking the grandeur of this magnificent city *(or town)* of yours has proved a restorative to my spirit. *(Beat, taking in the audience.)* Yes, to rise early and see the sun in all its splendor while we can, for his brightness seldom lasts the day through. The morning of the day and the morning of life are but too much alike: fail to take notice and dusk has with alacrity encroached on one's journey, signaling all too soon the day's end.

Well.

But our journey has yet to begin, so let us proceed.

HE TAKES A SIP OF WATER AND, WHEN READY, BEGINS HIS PERFORMANCE. HIS FIRST SELECTION, FROM THE PICKWICK PAPERS

Samuel Pickwick burst like another sun from his slumbers, threw open his chamber window, and looked out upon the world beneath. Goswell Street was at his feet, Goswell Street was on his right hand, and his left, and as far as the eye could reach.

"Such," thought Mr. Pickwick, "are the narrow views of those philosophers who, content only with examining the things that lie before them, look not to the truths which are hidden beyond."

And having given vent to this beautiful reflection, Mr. Pickwick proceeded to put himself into his clothes, and his clothes into his portmanteau. Great men are seldom over scrupulous in the arrangement of their attire; the operation of shaving, dressing, and coffee-imbibing was soon performed; and, in another hour, Mr. Pickwick, with his portmanteau in his hand, his telescope in his greatcoat pocket, and his note-book in his waistcoat, set out for adventure, ready for the reception of any discoveries worthy of being noted down.

On that first night's journey, punctual to five o'clock, arrived his dear friend, Mr. Tracey Tupman, and shortly afterwards, their dinners.

"What's that?" Mr. Pickwick inquired, as the waiter uncovered one of the dishes.

"Soles, sir."

"Soles! Capital fish. Indeed! Capital!"

"Glass of wine, Sir."

"With pleasure. Mr. Tupman?"

"Oh, yes, thank you, my friend."

"Quite a mess on the staircase there, waiter. Carpenters coming down — lamps, glasses, harps. What's going forward?"

"Ball, Sir. For the benefit of charity. Costume like. Fancy ball, sir."

"Many fine women in this town, do you know, sir?" inquired Mr. Tupman, with great interest.

"You might say that, sir."

"I should very much like to go, very much."

"Tickets at the bar, sir, half-a-guinea each, sir."

"I shall go as a bandit! In green velvet and tails!"

"What!"

"As a bandit."

"You don't mean to say," said Mr. Pickwick, gazing with solemn sternness at his friend — "you don't mean to say, Mr. Tupman, that it is your intention to put yourself into a green velvet jacket, with a two-inch tail?"

"Such IS my intention, Sir. And why not, sir?"

"Because, Sir, because you are too old, Sir."

"Too old!"

"And if any further ground of objection be wanting, you are too fat, sir."

"Sir," said Mr. Tupman, his face suffused with a crimson glow, "that is an insult."

"Sir, it is not half the insult to you, that your appearance in my presence in a green velvet jacket, with a two-inch tail, would be to me."

"Sir, you're a fellow!"

"Sir, you're another!"

Mr. Tupman advanced a step or two, and glared at Mr. Pickwick. Mr. Pickwick returned the glare, concentrated into a focus by means of his spectacles, and breathed a bold defiance.

"Sir, you have called me old."

"I have."

"And fat."

"I reiterate the charge."

"And a fellow."

"So you are!"

There was a fearful pause.

"My attachment to your person, sir, is great — very great — but upon that person, I must take summary vengeance."

"Come on, Sir!" replied Mr. Pickwick. Stimulated by the exciting nature of the dialogue, the heroic man actually threw himself into a paralytic attitude, confidently supposed by the waiter to have been intended as a posture of defense.

"Gentlemen!" exclaimed the waiter, suddenly recovering the power of speech and rushing between the two, at the imminent hazard of receiving an application on the temple from each — "what! Gentlemen, with the eyes of the world upon you! For shame, gentlemen; for shame."

The unwonted lines which momentary passion had ruled in Mr. Pickwick's clear and open brow, gradually melted away. His countenance resumed its usual benign expression.

"I have been hasty, very hasty. Tupman; your hand."

The dark shadow passed from Mr. Tupman's face, as he warmly grasped the hand of his friend.

"I have been hasty, too,"

"No, no, the fault was mine. You will wear the green velvet jacket?"

"No, no,"

"To oblige me, you will."

"Well, well, I will."

Thus Mr. Pickwick was led by the very warmth of his own good feelings to give his consent to a proceeding from which his better judgment would have recoiled – a more striking illustration of this great man's amiable character can hardly be conceived."

HIS FIRST SELECTION COMPLETE.

From *The Pickwick Papers.*

I have sometimes been accused of having more ability than taste.

The Posthumous Papers of the Pickwick Club was one of my very first works, appearing in a series of monthly installments. A publishing form scorned at the time as undignified and low. After the fourth installment monthly sales rose from four hundred to forty *thousand*.

And the race was on.

"Ride on! Roughshod if need be, smooth-shod if that will do, but ride on over all obstacles—and win the race!"

"And win what race?" asked young David Copperfield.

"Why, whatever race one has started in!"

And a glorious race it has been.

HE TAKES A SIP OF WATER. PUTS HIS SCRIPT DOWN BEFORE PROCEEDING.

It is hard to fathom that it has been twenty-five years since my first journey to the United States. Quite a sea-change has transpired. In both of us. I've had the pleasure of visiting many new and wonderful places on this trip—Boston, a beautiful city; New York, just as beautiful but by no means as clean; Washington . . . magnificent *intentions*; Philadelphia, a handsome city, but distractingly regular, after an hour of walking about I felt I would have given the world for a crooked street; indeed, the collar of my coat seemed to stiffen slightly beneath its Quakerly influence. And I will confess that the last venue in which I performed—which shall remain nameless—greeted me with such an air of academia that the evening seemed more suggestive of funeral baked meats than of festivities; like a Methodist Chapel in low spirits, with a cold in its head. A few blue people shivering.

No, nothing could be further from my wishes; and nothing could be more in accordance with them, than that we should make ourselves as like as possible to a small group of friends assembled to hear a tale told, and that we should at once forget anything ceremonious or formal in the manner of our coming together. For in the end, we are all merely players in one grand collective story, are we not? Each of us wondering what's going to happen next . . .

PLAYS THE PAUSE.

I know I am.

I am extremely anxious to see how this all turns out.

BEGINS HIS NEXT SELECTION.

Nicholas Nickleby and his troupe of traveling players proceeded along on their journey.

LEANS OVER THE PODIUM AS HE TRANSFORMS INTO MR. CRUMMLES, WHO IS SPEAKING TO HIS PONY.

"We're counting on you, lad! That's it—that's it! Almost there!"

The actor-manager, Mr. Vincent Crummles, and Nicholas, occupied the front seat of a vehicle of unknown design, on which Mr. Crummles bestowed the appellation of a "four wheeled phaeton." The rest of the players, and Smike, being packed behind, together with broad-swords, pistols, wigs, kingly costumes, and other professional necessaries.

THE PONY SITS IN THE ROAD.

"Oh, come, my good boy—once more now—for Harry and St. George!"

Mr. Crummles had a strange four-legged animal, which he called a pony, bridled before him. The pony took his time upon the road, and—possibly in consequence of his theatrical education—evinced, every now and then, a strong inclination to lie down

THE PONY DOES SO.

"He's a good pony at bottom," said Mr. Crummles to Nicholas. "Many and many is the circuit he has gone. He is quite one of us. His mother was on the stage."

"Oh. Was she?" rejoined Nicholas.

"Indeed she was. She ate apple-pie at a circus for upwards of fourteen years, "fired pistols, and went to bed in a nightcap. In short, she took to the low comedy entirely. His father was a dancer."

"Indeed. Was he at all distinguished?"

"Not very. *(So as not to let the pony hear.)* He was rather a *low* sort of pony. He was clever in comedy and the melodrama, but in the straight plays, the classics, too broad—too broad. When the mother died, the father took to the wine."

"The wine!"

"Aye. Drinking port-wine with the clown. But he was a greedy pony, and one night bit off the neck of the bottle and choked himself. So his vulgarity was the death of him at last."

SELECTION COMPLETE.

That of course from *The Life and Adventures of Nicholas Nickleby.*

ABOUT TO READ THE NEXT SELECTION. STOPS.

I know that such ventures as these are quite common now, but when I first began, very few writers had ever performed public readings. Many of my associates tried desperately to dissuade me from such an undertaking. I was warned it would be the ruin of my career—it would call into question my seriousness as a writer; descending to the vulgarity of the *stage*. Heaven forefend. I have been the beneficiary of an almost constant stream of 'advice' throughout my career. But as Mr. Kenwigs wisely asserts in *Nicholas Nickleby*: "A man in public life expects to be sneered at."

PICKS UP SCRIPT AGAIN.

And may I say—*ask*, rather—that if, as I proceed, you should feel further disposed to give some outward expression to any little emotions awakened by my readings *(meaning 'applause')*, I encourage you to do so without the least apprehension of disturbing me. After all, in life, as in the theater, one does need to know one is being heard.

LAUNCHES INTO HIS NEXT SELECTION.

"Being then in a pleasant frame of mind, I resolved to go to a play. And there, from the back of a centre box, I saw *Julius Caesar*. To have all those noble Romans alive before me, and walking in and out for my entertainment, instead of being the stern taskmasters they had been at school when reading them, was a most novel and delightful effect. But the mingled reality and mystery of the whole show, the influence upon me of the poetry, the lights, the music, were so dazzling, and opened up such illimitable regions of delight, that when I came out into the rainy street, at twelve o'clock at night, I felt as if I had come from the clouds, where I had been leading a romantic life for ages, to a bawling, splashing, link-lighted, umbrella-struggling, muddy, miserable world. I stood in the street for a little while, as if I really were a stranger upon earth. I was so . . . filled with the play."

SELECTION COMPLETE

David Copperfield.

BEAT.

I have always loved the theater. I actually began as an actor. A comic actor. Yes. I loved the clowns. Particularly in Shakespeare; very complicated writing—which I admire—very subversive writing too, which I *greatly* admire. As an actor I was regarded by many as much more than adequate. One night in particular I recall I was leaving the theater, when a patron passed me and said, 'Ah, Mr. Dickens, what an actor you would have made, if it just hadn't been for them books.'

Them books.

Although I may have forsaken my theatrical aspirations, I have never abandoned the theater; no, over and over again it has been my delight to take my seat in a theater such as this. Often sitting next to some grim-faced person, forced to attend, who settles in at first a mere figure of silent snow, but who gradually softens, begins to thaw, leans forward in his seat, his face aglow as he rides the crescendo of, “Once more unto the breach, dear friends, once more; Or close the wall up with our English dead!”

William Shakespeare. All writers humbly bow before his mighty genius.

HE READS.

"Oh, Shakespeare's an infernal humbug! What's the good of Shakespeare? I never read him! What the devil is he all about, anyway? There's a lot of feet in Shakespeare’s verse, but there ain't any legs worth mentioning in his plays, now are there? Juliet, Desdemona, Lady Macbeth, and all the rest of 'em, whatever their names are, might as well have no legs at all for anything the audience sees of ‘em. I'll tell you what it is. What the people call dramatic poetry these days is nothing but a collection of sermons. Do I go to the theatre to be lectured? No, I don’t. If I wanted that, I'd go to church! What's the legitimate object of the drama, I ask you? Human nature. What are legs? Human nature. Yes, human nature is what I comes to see!”

Martin Chuzzlewit.

Human nature, indeed, is the lifeblood of theater.

And my theater was upon the page.

HE ATTACKS A PASSAGE FROM HARD TIMES.

"Girl number twenty! I don't know that girl. Who is that girl?"

"Sissy Jupe, sir," explained number twenty, blushing.

"Sissy is not a name. Don't call yourself Sissy. Call yourself Cecilia."

"It's Father as calls me Sissy, Sir."

"Then he has no business to do it! Tell him he mustn't, *Cecilia Jupe.* What is your father?"

"He belongs to the horse-riding, if you please, sir."

Mr. Gradgrind waved off the objectionable calling. "We don't want to know anything about that here. Your father breaks horses, don't he?"

"If you please, sir, when they can get any to break."

"Very well, then. Describe your father as a horse breaker. Give me your definition of a horse."

"Well . . . I—

"Girl number twenty unable to define a horse! Girl number twenty possessed of no facts in reference to one of the commonest of animals! Some boy's definition of a horse. Bitzer, yours."

A young boy stood, so pale with grief at the prospect, that he looked as though, if he were cut, he would bleed white.

"Bitzer! Your definition of a horse."

"Quadruped. Graminivorous. Forty teeth, namely twenty-four grinders, and twelve incisor. Sheds coat in spring; in marshy countries, sheds hoofs too. Hoofs hard, but requiring to be shod with iron. Age known by marks in mouth."

"Now, girl number twenty, you know what a horse is. Sit. Now, let me ask you, girls and boys. Suppose you were going to carpet a room. Would you use a carpet having a representation of flowers upon it?"

There being a general conviction in the class that "No, sir!" was usually the right answer to this gentleman, the chorus of *"No!"* was very strong. Only a few feeble stragglers said yes; among them, Sissy Jupe.

"Girl number twenty."

Sissy blushed, and stood again.

"So you would carpet your room with representations of flowers. Why would you?"

"If you please sir, I am very fond of flowers."

"And is that why you would put tables and chairs upon them, and have people walking over them in heavy boots?"

"It wouldn't hurt them, sir. They wouldn't be real; they would just be pictures of what was pretty and pleasant, and I would fancy—"

"Ay, ay, ay! But you mustn't fancy! You must never Fancy! Fact, fact, fact! You are not to have, in any object of use or ornament, anything that would be a contradiction of fact. You don't walk upon flowers in *fact*; you cannot be allowed to walk upon flowers in *carpets*. What is called Taste is only another name for Fact. We hope to have before long, a board of fact composed of commissioners of fact, who will force the people to be people of fact, and of nothing but fact. If you wish to decorate your carpet, you must use combinations and modifications – in primary colors – of mathematical figures which are susceptible to proof and demonstration. This is a new principle, a new discovery, and a great one! This is Fact. This is Taste! You must discard the word Fancy altogether!"

PUNCTUATES THIS ENDING BY SLAMMING A BOOK DOWN OR SOME SUCH ACTION.

From *Hard Times.*

HIS PERSONAL FEELINGS RISING SLIGHTLY TO THE SURFACE.

Yes, Mr. Gradgrind; a man of facts and calculations; with a rule and a pair of scales always in his pocket, ready to weigh and measure any parcel of human nature and tell you exactly what it's worth. *(He flips through his script.)* Would that he were merely a fiction. A society without Fancy, without imagination, never did, never can, and never will, hold a great place under the sun. Without imagination, there can be no compassion.

ABOUT TO CONTINUE, WHEN HE DECIDES TO CHOOSE A DIFFERENT SELECTION THAN MIGHT EXPRESS WHAT HE IS FEELING MORE ADEQUATELY. HE SEARCHES – FINDS A SELECTION. READS FROM OLIVER TWIST.

Although I am not disposed to maintain that being born in a workhouse is in itself the most enviable circumstance that can befall a human being, I do mean to say that it was the best thing that could have occurred for *Oliver Twist*. The fact is, that there was considerable difficulty in inducing the infant Oliver to take upon him the office of respiration—and for some time he lay gasping on a little flock mattress, rather unequally poised between this world and the next. Now, if during this brief period, Oliver had been surrounded by anxious aunts, experienced nurses, and doctors of profound wisdom, he would most inevitably have been killed in no time. There being nobody by, however, but a pauper woman, who was rendered rather misty by an unwonted allowance of beer, Oliver and Nature fought out the point between them. The result was, that, after a few struggles, Oliver breathed, sneezed, and proceeded, by way of a loud cry, to advertise to the inmates of the workhouse the fact of a new *burden* having been imposed upon them. He was badged, ticketed, and put into his place at once—the orphan of a workhouse—a parish child.

Oliver cried lustily.

If he could have known that he was an orphan, left to the tender mercies of churchwardens, perhaps he would have cried the louder.

Sevenpence—

STOPS READING TO ADD A COMMENT.

Lest there should be any well-intentioned persons who do not perceive in my writings the difference between true religion and hypocrisy, between piety and the pretense of piety, let them know that it always the latter, and never the former which I satirize. Further, that which I satirize is inconsistent with true piety, incapable of union with it, and one of the most evil and mischievous falsehoods existing in society—whether it establish its headquarters behind the doors of an orphanage, a chapel, or the halls of our great Capitols.

CONTINUES.

Sevenpence halfpenny a week can provide a good round diet for a child; quite enough to overload its stomach and make it uncomfortable. The elderly female in charge of Oliver was a woman of wisdom and experience; she knew what was good for children. So, she appropriated the greater part of the weekly stipend to her own use, thereby, finding in the lowest depth a deeper still.

STOPS AGAIN.

It may appear unnecessary to once again offer a word of observation on so plain a head, but nevertheless, I say without apology, that it is never out of season to protest against that coarse familiarity with sacred things which is busy on the lip and idle in the heart; or against any class of persons who have just enough religion to make them hate, and not enough to make them love one another.

RESUMES.

Oliver's ninth birthday found him a pale, thin child, somewhat diminutive in stature, and decidedly small in circumference. He was keeping his birthday in the coal-cellar when Mrs. Mann, the lady of the house, was unexpectedly startled by the apparition of Mr. Bumble, the parish beadle, striving to undo the garden gate.

"Goodness gracious! Is that you, Mr. Bumble, sir?—(Susan, take Oliver upstairs and wash 'em directly!)—My heart alive, Mr. Bumble, how glad I am to see you! Walk in, sir; walk in, I pray, Mr. Bumble, sir."

"Do you think this respectful or proper conduct, Mrs. Mann? To keep the parish officer a-waiting when I come here upon parochial business connected with the parochial orphans?"

"Oh, pardon me, sir. I was jus' tellin' the dear children as is so fond of you, that it was you was coming."

"Well. It may be as you say. It may be. Lead the way."

Mrs. Mann ushered the beadle into a small parlor.

"Now don't be offended by what I'm a-going to say. You've had a long walk, you know, or I wouldn't mention it. Now, will you take a little drop of somethink, Mr. Bumble?"

"Not a drop. Not a drop."

"Just a wee bit, with a little cold water, 'n a lump o' sugar. I'm obliged to keep a bit in the house—for the children, sir, when theys sick."

"What is it?"

"It's gin. I'll not deceive you, Mr. B. It's gin. For the blessed infants, sir; I can't bears to see them suffer."

"You are a humane woman, Mrs. Mann." (Here she set down the glass.) I shall take an opportunity of mentioning it to the board. (He drew it towards him.) You feel as a mother, Mrs. Mann. (He stirred the gin and water.) "I drink your health with cheerfulness, Mrs. Mann," and he swallowed half of it. "Now, I should like to observe the children at supper."

"Aye, sir, aye. This way, Mr. Bumble."

The room in which the boys were fed was a large stone hall with a great copper pot at one end, out of which the cook ladled the gruel. Each boy had one serving, and no more, after which, they would sit staring at the great copper pot as if they could have devoured up the very bricks on which it sat. Oliver Twist and his companions became so wild with hunger that one boy hinted darkly that unless he had another basin of gruel, he was afraid he might some night happen to eat the boy who slept next to him. He had a manic, hungry eye, and they explicitly believed him. A council was held; lots were cast who should walk up to the master and ask for more; and it fell to Oliver Twist.

The boys whispered to each other, and winked at Oliver, while his neighbors nudged him. Child as he was, he was desperate with hunger. He rose from the table, and advancing to the cook, bowl and spoon in hand, said, somewhat alarmed at his own temerity:

"Please, sir, I want some more."

The cook was a fat healthy man, but he turned very pale. He gazed in stupefied astonishment on the small rebel for some seconds, and then clung to the copper pot for support.

"What!"

"Please, sir, I want some more."

The cook aimed a blow at Oliver's head with the ladle, and pinioned his arms. "I beg pardon, sir, but Oliver Twist has asked for more!"

Mrs. Mann shrieked aloud. "For *more*

"*More*, did you say?! Do I understand that this boy asked for *more*, after he had eaten the parochial portion allotted by the parochial dietary!"

"*(Cook.)* He did! Profane monster!"

"*(Mrs. Mann.)* Impious ingrate!"

"Lock him up this instant! Lock him up and prevent the other children from falling prey to the sins of one who is obviously under the powers of wickedness, and an article direct from the Devil himself!"

SELECTION COMPLETE. THE ENERGY OF THIS LAST READING HAS TAKEN A BIT OUT OF HIM. HE TRIES NOT TO SHOW IT. THIS WILL BECOME MORE DIFFICULT AS THE EVENING PROCEEDS – PARTICULARLY IN THE SELECTIONS WHICH TAKE MORE OUT OF HIM, OR ONES WHERE HE CANNOT HELP BUT BECOME MORE EMOTIONALLY INVOLVED IN.

When I completed Oliver Twist, I fully expected it would be objected to on some very high moral grounds in some very high moral quarters. Of these self-appointed standard bearers of Morality, let me simply say, that I have no respect for their opinion, good or bad, do not covet their approval, and do not write for their amusement—these insects of the hour who raise their little hum, and beat their wings, and die forgotten—

I begin to wax political. Forgive me.

My doctors have warned me about that.

"Beg pardon," as Sam Weller said, "but when I gets on this here grievance, I runs on like a new barrow with the wheel jus' greased."

ABOUT TO CONTINUE, BUT UNABLE TO STOP HIMSELF

And yet, I satirize these public figures and institutions—forgive me—I satirize them not because I and the rest of mankind are devoid of such oppressive tendencies, but because the self-indulgence and lack of compassion in public figures directly effects the lives of so many innocents—the young, the old, the infirm. I learned as a mere boy to hold suspect those whose moral and religious beliefs conveniently coincide with their own earthly goals—and then there are those of so refined and delicate a nature that they cannot bear to contemplate the horrors of this world, and therefore feel that no one else should contemplate them either. I have no faith in the delicacy that cannot bear to look upon the truth. I myself have known what it is to have no hope—that is no matter—there is nothing delicate about poverty, or its causes, or the horrors which it breeds.

HE READS FROM FROM OLIVER TWIST. SOMEWHERE DURING THIS SELECTION, HE PUTS THE SCRIPT DOWN AS HE BECOMES EMOTIONALLY INVOLVED AND ACTS THE SCENE OUT FULLY, PERHAPS LEAVING THE PODIUM AND TAKING THE STAGE.

Without one pause, the robber, Bill Sikes, held on his headlong course, until he reached his own door. He opened it, softly, with a key; strode lightly up the stairs; and entering his own room, double-locked the door, and lifted a heavy table against it. The dog, who'd been following at his heels, scurried into the corner as Sikes flung back the curtain of the bed.

Nancy was lying, half-dressed, upon it. He had roused her from her sleep, for she raised herself with a hurried and startled look.

"Get up!"

"It is you, Bill!" said the girl, with an expression of pleasure at his return.

"It is. Get up."

There was a candle burning, but the man hastily drew it from the candlestick, and hurled it under the grate. Seeing the faint light of early day without, the girl rose to undraw the curtain.

"Let it be, there's light enough for wot I've got to do."

"Bill, why do you look like that at me!"

The robber sat regarding her, for a few seconds, with dilated nostrils and heaving breast; and then, grasping her by the head and throat, dragged her into the middle of the room, and looking once towards the door, placed his heavy hand upon her mouth.

"Bill, Bill! I—I won't scream or cry not once—hear me—speak to me—tell me what I've done!"

"You know, you she-devil. You were watched tonight; every word you said was heard."

"I didn't tell them nothing about you! Bill, dear Bill, you cannot have the heart to kill me. You shall have time to think and save yourself this crime; I will not loose my hold! I have been true to you, upon my guilty soul I have!"

The man struggled violently to release his arms; but those of the girl were clasped round his, and tear as he would, he could not tear them away.

"Bill, the gentleman and that dear lady told me tonight of a home where I could end my days in peace. Let me see them again and beg them to show the same mercy to you; then we can both of us leave this dreadful place. It's never too late to repent, but we must have time—a little, little time!"

Sikes freed one arm, and grasped his pistol. The certainty of immediate detection if he fired, flashed across his mind even in the midst of his fury; and he beat it twice with all the force he could summon, upon the upturned face that almost touched his own.

She staggered and fell, nearly blinded with the blood that rained down from a deep gash in her forehead, but raising herself, with difficulty, on her knees, folded her hands before her, as high towards Heaven as her feeble strength would allow and breathed one prayer for mercy.

It was a ghastly figure to look upon. The murderer staggering backward to the wall, and shutting out the sight with his hand, seized a heavy club and struck her down.

PAUSE.

Of all the bad deeds that, under cover of the darkness, had been committed within wide London's bounds since night hung over it, that was the worst. Of all the horrors that rose with an ill scent upon the morning air, that was the foulest and most cruel. The sun burst upon the crowded city in clear and radiant glory. It lighted up the room where the murdered woman lay. If the sight had been a ghastly one in the dull morning, what was it now, in all that brilliant light!

The murderer had not moved; he had been afraid to stir. There had been a moan and motion of the girl's hand; and, with terror added to rage, he had struck and struck again. Once he threw a rug over it; but it was worse to imagine the eyes moving towards him. He had plucked it off again. And there was the body – mere flesh and blood, no more – but such flesh, and so much blood!

He struck a light, kindled a fire, and thrust the club into it. There was hair upon the end, which blazed and shrunk into a light cinder, and, caught by the air, whirled up the chimney. He held the weapon till it broke, and then piled it on the coals to burn away. He washed himself, and rubbed his clothes; there were spots that would not be removed, but he cut the pieces out, and burnt them. How those stains were dispersed about the room! The very feet of the dog were bloody.

All this time he had never once turned his back upon the corpse, no, not for a moment. He moved backwards toward the door, dragging the dog with him lest he should soil his feet anew and carry evidence of the crime into the streets. He shut the door softly, locked it, took the key, and left the house.

PAUSE. HE IS EXHAUSTED AND WEAKENED BY THE READING.

Oliver Twist.

HE TAKES A BRIEF MOMENT TO RECOVER.

I have been a good deal criticized for often depicting in great detail what is wrong with certain systems in our society, but never offering any alternatives to them. I am glad to have had my books challenged, for in that circumstance alone I find a sufficient assurance that they needed to be written.

Holding a light upon society's faults may not be the answer, but, dear heavens, we all know it is a beginning!

Pause.

However . . . ladies and gentlemen . . . I find myself in need of a short interval . . . Perhaps we all might take a moment to refresh ourselves—*refresh*—to be fresh again. *(He looks about.)* How extraordinary. I can see every one of your dear faces. And that is everything, is it not?

To see one another fully.

Excuse me.

HE EXITS.

END OF ACT 1

ACT TWO

DICKENS ENTERS TO PODIUM, SCRIPT IN HAND. VERY SERIOUS.

Ode to an Expiring Frog.

QUITE GRAVELY.

Can I view thee panting, lying
On thy stomach, without sighing;
Can I unmoved see thee dying
On a log,
Expiring frog.

(The next verse is more touching still.)

Say, have fiends in shape of boys,
With wild halloo, and brutal noise
Hunted thee from marshy joys
With a dog,
Expiring frog!

(Enjoying the humor of the piece.) Mrs. Leo Hunter's poem as recited in *The Pickwick Papers.*

Before proceeding, I should like to say something. I have not been entirely forthright with you this evening. Due to certain issues of health, of a long-standing nature, I have decided to cease forever my public readings, to cancel those which lie before me, and to return again to England.

In this brief life it is indeed sad to say one is doing *any*thing for the last time. Be that as it may . . . this is the last time I will appear before you, or any of my reading public.

Hence, many of these passages tonight seem to have taken on a somewhat deeper resonance for me. You must understand that from the beginning I have been nearly obsessed with what I perceive as the injustices of this world—and I still am today, perhaps even more so—because tragically these injustices still exist; and here I am at the end of my . . . journey, and they hover about me this evening—taunting me, "A lifetime of writing against us. Pity."

A lifetime.

Even as a schoolboy—I thought the very words assigned to the letters of the *alphabet* were unjust.

RECITING FROM MEMORY. SPEAKING AS A CHILD.

"'A' was an archer who shot a frog. Of course 'A' was an Archer. He was an Apple-pie and Anteater also! He was a good many things in his time, was 'A'. And so were his friends, except 'X', who had so little versatility that I never knew him to get beyond Xerxes or Xantippe—and poor 'Y', who was always confined to a Yacht or a Yew tree; and 'Z' condemned for ever to be a Zebra or a Zany."

That was my mother's alphabet—I can still see the fat black letters. *(Beat.)* My mother. If nothing else, she did teach me to read . . .

Changing the subject.

My father, although he spent money on nearly everything than that which he should have been spending it on, did make a few purchases, for which I am ever grateful. He acquired a very small collection of books that he stored in the attic, which we cheekily called the Library: *Roderick Randon*, *Peregrine Pickle*, *The Vicar of Wakefield*. From that glorious attic they came to me, a host of friends when I had no single friend, to keep a small and sickly boy company.

RECITING FROM MEMORY.

"My latht wordth on the thubject ith thith. People mutht be amuthed thomehow. They can't be alwayth a working, nor yet they can't be alwayth a learning. We muth make the betht of ith; not the wurtht. I conthider that I lay down the philothophy of the thubject when I thay to you, make the betht of ith: not the wurtht!"

Mr. Sleary from *Hard Times.*

We must make the best of it, mustn't we. *(Beat.)* I have never before spoken in public of my family, nor my upbringing. Suddenly, I find myself compelled to deviate from that principle which I have so long observed. I must say, it does make one feel a bit like a beast in a caravan describing himself in the keeper's absence, but . . .

SEARCHING A MOMENT.

I may tell you without any fear, that I was born. My father was in the Navy Pay Office; we moved quite often when I was young . . . and I remember thinking life sloppier than I had expected to find it. I need not delve too deeply into the history of my father's arrest for debt, our constant evictions, nor our experiences in debtors' prison. Suffice it to say, my father had great expectations, but not the means to accomplish them.

He was a better man than I thought him. As many fathers often are.

My carefree days ended at the age of eleven when I was taken out of school and sent away from my family, to live on my own. My mother never once objected, being entirely satisfied with my situation. Indeed, she encouraged it. I was put to work in a blacking factory—pasting labels upon jars of boot-polish. It is still wonderful to me how a boy could have been so easily cast away at such an age. My whole nature was so penetrated with this experience, that even now, famous and caressed and happy, I often, in my dreams, wander desolately back to that time of my life . . .

HE RECITES FROM MEMORY.

"Here are no canterings or moonlight heaths, no merry-makings in the snuggest of all possible caverns, none of the attractions of dress, no embroidery, no lace. The cold wet shelterless midnight streets of London; the foul and frowsy dens, where vice is closely packed and lacks the room to turn; the *workhouse*; the haunts of hunger and disease; the tattered rags that scarcely hold together are all that you shall find here."

Oliver Twist.

I know that I worked from morning till night, a shabby child; that I was often too frightened to sleep; that I have lounged in the streets insufficiently fed; and I know that, but for the mercy of God, I might just as easily have been a thief or a vagabond; a Fagin, or a Dodger.

I do not think resentfully or angrily upon my past, for I know all these things have worked together to make me what I am, but I have never forgotten. Indeed, had I but one wish, it would be that every parent—every King and Queen, for that matter, every President and Ruler, might go to school to their own laws, might know hunger and hopelessness, or at least make the effort to *imagine* them and so learn compassion.

BEAT.

I married—*am* married—to the daughter of a writer. Our marriage, despite the rumors of feeble-minded gossip-mongers –

HE STOPS HIMSELF. DECIDING NOT TO EXPOUND ON THIS, HE CHANGES THE SUBJECT.

I have eleven children, one with God; I have been liberally recompensed throughout my career and handsomely acknowledged; I have a roost dogs; and am delighted to view any sports in which the impotent effects of unskillful people do not endanger human life.

I love to walk.

And here I am. *(Beat. Holding up the manuscript or book.)* And *here* I am.

"Whether I shall turn out to be the hero of my own life, or whether that station shall be held by anybody else, these pages must show."

Anyone? *David Copperfield.*

HE FLIPS THROUGH THE PAGES, MUSING ON HIS LIFE'S WORK.

It has been observed that you cannot judge of an author's personal character from his writings. It may be that you cannot—I think it is very likely, for many reasons, that you cannot—but, at least, a reader will rise from the perusal of a book with some defined and tangible idea of the writer's moral creed and broad purpose.

CHOOSING WITH PURPOSE THE NEXT SELECTION.

And on that point . . .

HE LAUNCHES ENTHUSIASTICALLY INTO A CHRISTMAS CAROL.

"Oh! But he was a tight-fisted hand at the grindstone, Scrooge! A squeezing, wrenching, grasping, scraping, clutching, covetous old sinner! Hard and sharp as flint, from which no steel had ever struck out generous fire; secret, and self-contained, and solitary as an oyster. The cold within him froze his old features, nipped his pointed nose, shriveled his cheek, stiffened his gait; made his eyes red, his thin lips blue; and spoke out shrewdly in his grating voice. A frosty rime was on his head, and on his eyebrows, and his wiry chin. He carried his own low temperature always about with him; he iced his office in the dog-days; and didn't thaw it one degree at Christmas.

"A merry Christmas, uncle! God save you!" cried a cheerful voice. It was the voice of Scrooge's nephew, Fred, who came to the counting house.

"Bah! Humbug!"

"Christmas a humbug, uncle! You don't mean that, I am sure?"

"I do!" said Scrooge. "Merry Christmas! What right have you to be merry? You're poor enough."

"Come, then, what right have you to be dismal? You're rich enough."

"Humbug!"

"Don't be cross, uncle."

"What else can I be when I live in such a world of fools as this. Merry Christmas! Out upon merry Christmas! What's Christmas time to you but a time for paying bills without money; a time for finding yourself a year older, but not an hour richer. If I could work my will, every idiot who goes about with 'Merry Christmas' on his lips, should be boiled with his own pudding, and buried with a stake of holly through his heart!"

"Uncle!"

"Nephew! Keep Christmas in your own way me keep it in mine."

"Keep it! But you don't keep it."

"Then let me leave it alone then! Much good may it do you! Much good has it ever done you!"

"There are many things from which I have derived good, by which I have not profited, Uncle. And though Christmas has never put a scrap of gold in my pocket, I believe it *has* done me good, and *will* do me good, and I say, God bless it!"

The clerk in the back room involuntarily applauded.

"Let me hear another word from you, Bob Cratchit, and you'll keep your Christmas by losing your situation. You're a powerful speaker, sir. I wonder you don't go into Parliament."

"Don't be angry, uncle. Come! Dine with us tomorrow."

"I'd rather die."

"I want nothing from you; I ask nothing of you; why cannot we be friends?"

"Good afternoon."

"I am sorry, with all my heart, to find you so resolute. But I have made the trial in homage to Christmas, and I'll keep my Christmas humor to the last. So a Merry Christmas, uncle!"

"Humbug."

"And a Happy New Year!"

"Good afternoon!"

STOPS TO ADD A COMMENT.

Ladies and gentlemen, my moral creed is very easily summed up. I have faith, and I wish to express that faith in the celebration of beautiful things, and in the revelation of oppressive and horrible things.

CONTINUES.

The Ghost of Christmas Past stopped and gestured to Scrooge.

"Do you know this place?" it asked.

They had stopped at a certain warehouse door.

"Know it! Why I was apprenticed here!" They went in. An old gentleman sat behind a desk, working. "Why, it's old Fezziwig! Bless his heart; it's Fezziwig alive again!"

Old Fezziwig looked up at the clock, rubbed his hands; adjusted his capacious waistcoat and called out in a comfortable, oily, rich, fat, jovial voice:

"Yo ho, there! Ebenezer! Dick!" Scrooge's former self, a young man, came briskly in, accompanied by his fellow apprentice. "Yo ho, my boys! No more work tonight. Christmas Eve, Ebenezer! Let's have the shutters up before a man can say Jack Robinson."

You wouldn't believe how those two young fellows went at it! They charged into the street with the shutters—one, two, three—had 'em up in their places—four, five, six—barred 'em and pinned 'em—seven eight nine—and came back in panting like race horses.

"Let's clear away now, my lads. That's it, let's have lots of room here!"

It was done in a minute; the floor was swept and watered, the lamps were trimmed, fuel was heaped upon the fire; and the warehouse was as snug, and warm, and bright a ballroom as you would desire to see upon a winter's night.

In came a fiddler who made an orchestra of himself and tuned up like fifty stomach-aches. In came Mrs. Fezziwig, one vast substantial smile. In came three Miss Fezziwigs, beaming and lovable. In came six young followers whose hearts they broke. In came all the young men and women employed in the business. In came the housemaid, with her cousin, the baker. In came the cook, with her brother's friend, the milkman. In came the boy from across the way, and the girl from next door. In they all came, one after another; some shyly, some boldly, some gracefully, some awkwardly, some pushing, some pulling; in they all came anyhow and everyhow! And then away they all went twenty couples dancing at once, hands half round, and back again the other way; down the middle and up again; over and over, until the fiddler struck up the Roger de Coverly. Then old Fezziwig stood up to dance with Mrs. Fezziwig. A positive light appeared to issue from Fezziwig's calves. They shone in every part of the dance like moons. You couldn't have predicted, at any time, what would become of 'em next!

During the whole time, Scrooge had acted like a man out of his wits. His heart and soul were in the scene. He watched as his former self and two other apprentices, breathless and laughing, poured out their hearts in praise of old Fezziwig. It was then that Scrooge became conscious of the Ghost looking full upon him.

"What is the matter, Ebenezer?"

". . . Nothing particular."

"Something, I think?"

"No. No. I should like to be able to say a word or two to my clerk, Bob Cratchit, just now. That's all."

HE STOPS AGAIN.

It is very difficult to sum up a life's work, but if pressed to, I would have to say very simply that I have always had, and still have, an earnest desire to increase our stock of harmless cheerfulness and enjoyment. And dare I say: hope.

CONTINUES.

The three Spirits were now gone and Scrooge awoke in his own room! The bed was his own, the curtains were his own. Best and happiest of all, the Time before him was his own, to make amends in.

"I don't know what day of the month it is! I don't know how long I've been among the Spirits. I don't know anything. I'm quite a baby. Never mind. I don't care. I'd rather *be* a baby!"

Scrooge's hands were busy with his garments all this time; turning them inside out, putting them on upside down, tearing them, mislaying them. Running to the window, he opened it, and put out his head. "What's to-day?" he called down to a boy in Sunday clothes.

"Eh?"

"What's to-day, my fine fellow?"

"To-day?! Why, it's Christmas Day!"

"It's Christmas Day. I haven't missed it! The Spirits have done it all in one night! They can do anything they like! Of course they can. Of course they can. Hallo, my fine fellow!"

"Hallo."

"Do you know the butcher's shop, in the next street, at the corner?"

"Well, I should hope I do!"

"—an intelligent boy, a remarkable boy—Do you know whether they've sold the prize turkey that was hanging up there? Not the little prize turkey: the big one."

"What, the one as big as me?"

"—what a delightful boy; it's a pleasure to talk to him—Yes, my buck!"

"Why, it's hanging there now."

"Go and buy it."

"Go on!"

"No, no, I am in earnest. Go and buy it, and tell them to bring it here, that I may give them direction where to take it. Come back with the man, and I'll give you a shilling; come back with him in less than five minutes and I'll give you half a crown."

The boy was off like a shot.

"I'll send it to Bob Cratchit's. He shan't know who sends it. It's twice the size of Tiny Tim!"

When the boy returned, Scrooge rushed down-stairs and opened the street door. It was a turkey! He never could have stood upon his legs, that bird. He would have snapped them off in a minute, like sticks of sealing-wax.

"Why, it's impossible to carry that, my boy. You must have a cab."

The chuckle with which Scrooge said this, and the chuckle with which he paid for the Turkey, and the chuckle with which he paid for the cab, and the chuckle with which he recompensed the boy, were only to be exceeded by the chuckle with which he sat down breathless in his chair again, and chuckled till he cried.

Shaving was not an easy task, for his hand continued to shake very much; and shaving requires attention, even when you don't dance while you are at it. He dressed himself all in his best, and at last got out into the streets. He went to church, and watched the people hurrying to and fro, and patted children on the head, and questioned beggars, and found that everything could yield him pleasure. In the afternoon he turned his steps towards his nephew's house. He passed the door a dozen times, before he had the courage to go up and knock

KNOCKS.

"Why bless my soul," cried Fred, "who's that?"

"It's I. Your uncle Scrooge. I have come to dinner. Will you let me in, Fred?"

Let him in? Why, it was a mercy Fred didn't shake his arm off

Scrooge felt at home in five minutes. Wonderful party, wonderful games, wonderful happiness

But Scrooge was early at the office next morning. Oh, he was early there. If he could only be there first, and catch Bob Cratchit coming late. That was the thing he had set his heart upon. And he did it; yes, he did. The clock struck nine. No Bob. A quarter past. No Bob. He was full eighteen minutes and a half behind his time. Scrooge sat with his door wide open, that he might see him come into the counting house. Bob's hat was off, before he opened the door; his comforter too. He was on his stool in a jiffy; driving away with his pen, as if he were trying to overtake nine o'clock.

"What do you mean by coming here at this time of day."

"I am very sorry, sir. I am behind my time."

"You are. Yes. I think you are. Step this way, sir, if you please."

"It's only once a year, sir. It shall not be repeated. I was making rather merry yesterday, sir."

"Now, I'll tell you what, my friend. I am not going to stand this sort of thing any longer. And therefore," he continued, leaping from his stool, and giving Bob such a dig in the waistcoat that he staggered backward, "and therefore . . . I am about to . . . raise your salary!"

Bob trembled, and got a little nearer the fireplace poker. He had a momentary idea of knocking Scrooge down with it, holding him, and calling for help and a straight-jacket.

"A merry Christmas, Bob. A merrier Christmas, Bob, my good fellow, than I have given you for many a year. I'll raise your salary, and endeavor to assist your struggling family, and we will discuss your affairs this very afternoon."

Scrooge was better than his word. He did it all, and infinitely more. He became a good friend, a good master, and a good man; and ever afterwards, it was always said of him that he knew how to keep Christmas well, if any man alive possessed the knowledge. Some people laughed to see the alteration in him, but he let them laugh, and little heeded them; for he was wise enough to know that nothing ever happened on this globe, for good, at which some people did not have their fill of laughter at the outset; his own heart laughed: and that was quite enough for Scrooge."

SELECTION COMPLETE.

A Christmas Carol.

Christmas Carol. Perhaps the greatest success, I am told, that this ruffian and rascal has ever achieved. I was moved in the most extraordinary manner during its composition, walking the streets of London many a night—fifteen, twenty miles—when all of the sober folks had gone to bed, weeping, laughing, and weeping again as the story came to me.

It has been remarked—critically—that I have contributed greatly to the *lighter* literature of the world. I readily embrace the judgment, and, in fact, hold it dear. Yes . . . simple though they may be, I do believe these tales help to keep us, in some sense, ever young, by preserving through our worldly ways one slender track not overgrown with weeds, where we may walk again as children.

And now, ladies and gentlemen, dear friends, one last story, if I may.

My very last.

I feel like Prospero about to abjure his magic.

HE RECITES, FROM MEMORY, A CHILD'S STORY.

Once upon a time . . . a good many years ago, there was a traveler who set out upon a journey. It was a magic journey, and was to seem very long when he began it, and very short when he got half way through. He traveled along a rather dark path for some little time, without meeting anything, until at last he came to a beautiful child. So he said to the child, "What do you do here?" And the child said, "I am always at play. Come and play with me!"

So, he played with that child, the whole day long, and they were very merry. The sky was so blue, the sun was so bright, the water was so sparkling. They had plenty of the finest toys in the world, and the most astonishing picture-books: all about scimitars and slippers, and turbans and giants, blue-beards and bean-stalks: and all new and all true.

But, one day, of a sudden, the traveler lost the child. He called to him over and over again, but got no answer. So, he went upon his journey, and went on for a little while without meeting anything, until at last he came to a handsome boy. So, he said to the boy, "What do you do here?" And the boy said, "I am always learning. Come and learn with me."

So he learned with that boy about Jupiter and Juno, and the Greeks and the Romans, and I don't know what, and learned more than I could tell – or he either, for he soon forgot a great deal of it. But, they were not always learning; they had the merriest games that ever were played: hare and hounds, follow the leader, and more sports than I can think of; nobody could beat them. They had holidays too, and parties where they danced till midnight. As to friends, they had so many dear friends, and they were all young, like the handsome boy, and were never to be strange to one another all their lives through.

Still, one day, in the midst of all these pleasures, the traveler lost the boy as he had lost the child, and, after calling to him in vain, went on upon his journey. So he went on for a little while without meeting anything, until at last he came to a young man. So, he said to the young man, "What do you do here?" And the young man said, "I am always in love. Come and love with me."

So, he went away with that young man, and presently they came to one of the prettiest girls that ever was seen. So, the young man fell in love directly. Well! he was teased sometimes, and they quarreled sometimes, and they made it up, and wrote letters every day, and were always looking out for one another and pretending not to, and were engaged at Christmas-time, and were going to be married very soon!

But, the traveler lost them one day, as he had lost the rest of his friends, and, after calling to them to come back, which they never did, went on upon his journey. So, he went on for a little while without meeting anything, until at last he came to a middle-aged gentleman. So, he said to the gentleman, "What do you do here?" And his answer was, "I am always busy. Come and be busy with me!"

So, he began to be very busy with that gentleman, and they went on through the wood together. Now the whole journey had been through a wood, only it had been open and green at first, like a wood in spring; and now began to be thick and dark. The gentleman was not alone, but had a lady of about the same age with him, who was his wife; and they had many children, who were with them too. So, they all went on together through the wood, cutting down the trees, and making a path through the branches and the fallen leaves, and carrying burdens, and working very hard.

Then they came to a long green avenue that opened into deeper woods and then they all stood still, and one of the children said, "Father, I am going to sea," and another said, "Father, I am going to India," and another, "Father, I am going to seek my fortune where I can," and another, "Father, I am going to Heaven!" So, with many tears at parting, they went, solitary, down those avenues, each child upon its way.

Whenever these partings happened, the traveler looked at the gentleman, and saw him glance up at the sky above the trees, where the day was beginning to decline, and the sunset to come on. He saw, too, that his hair was turning grey. But, they never could rest long, for they had their journey to perform, and it was necessary for them to be always busy.

At last, there had been so many partings that there were no children left, and only the traveler, the gentleman, and the lady, went upon their way in company. And now the wood was yellow; and now brown; and the leaves of the trees began to fall. So, they came to an avenue that was darker than the rest, and were pressing forward on their journey without looking down it when the lady stopped.

"My husband," said the lady. "I am called."

They listened, and they heard a voice a long way down the avenue, say,

"Mother, mother!"

It was the voice of their child who had said, "I am going to Heaven!" and the father said, "I pray, my dear, not yet. The sunset is very near. Not yet, dearest!"

But, the mother, who was already drawn into the shade of the dark avenue and moving away with her arms still round his neck, kissed him, and said, "My dearest, I am summoned, and I must go!" And she was gone. And the traveler and he were left alone together.

And they went on and on together, until they came to very near the end of the wood: so near, that they could see the sunset shining red before them through the trees.

Yet, once more, while he broke his way among the branches, the traveler lost his friend. He called and called, but there was no reply, and when he passed out of the wood, and saw the peaceful sun going down upon a wide purple prospect, he came to an old man sitting on a fallen tree. So, he said to the old man, "What do you do here?" And the old man said with a calm smile, "I am always remembering. Come and remember with me . . . "

HE HAS FINISHED.

Thank you, my friends, for remembering with me.

THE END

FIRST PRODUCTION

Dickens in America was first produced at American Players Theater, directed by C. Michael Wright. Mr. Dickens was played by James Ridge. Costume design was by Holly Payne; scenic design, Nate Stuber; lighting design Noele Stollmack; stage manager, Erin Albrecht.

NOTES

Charles Dickens visited America twice in his life. When he first came here in 1842, he was a fairly young writer of 30, but his literary career was in full swing. He had already penned *The Pickwick Papers, Oliver Twist* and *Nicholas Nickleby.* The outspoken Dickens caused quite a bit of controversy at that time when he criticized Americans for, among other things, their lack of copyright laws.

Dickens was not only a natural storyteller, he was also a remarkable mimic. Having been drawn to the theatre earlier in his life, he had actually considered a career as an actor. His family said, while he was writing a novel, he would often spend hours in front of a mirror working out the face and the stance of a character. So it was only natural that he would take to the stage in 1853, the forerunner in a long line of novelists who presented public readings of their works.

By the time of his second visit to America in 1867, Dickens had become famous for his public readings and a lengthy tour had been scheduled. Sadly, his health was beginning to fail, so the tour had to be cut short. He never made it to the Midwest as planned.

We set out to rectify that unfortunate turn of events when we began to develop this piece. We decided to bring Charles Dickens back to America for a special visit, his final public reading. We combined a lot of fact with a little bit of fiction. Our Dickens is still a vibrant performer of his literary works and a passionate advocate for social reform. But beneath his stoicism and bravado, we can see glimpses of an extremely vulnerable man assessing the successes and the failures of a very full and complicated life.

—C. Michael Wright, director of the first production

OTHER PLAYS BY JAMES DEVITA

ADULT
An Improbable Fiction
Christmas in Babylon
Learning to Stay
Gift of the Magi
Cyrano De Bergerac
In Acting Shakespeare

YOUTH AND FAMILY
Alex and the Amazing Lemonade Stand
A Midnight Cry
Rose of Treason
Trials: the story of Joan of Arc, and Beth
Looking Glass Land
Excavating Mom
The Thief Lord
The Christmas Angel
A Little House Christmas
Treasure Island
Wonderland!
Arthur: The Boy Who Would Be King
The Prince and the Pauper
Tom Sawyer
Huckleberry Finn
The Three Musketeers
Swiss Family Robinson

For complete listings and details of Plays, please visit:
https://www.jamesdevita.com/playwrighting

ABOUT THE AUTHOR

James DeVita, a native of Long Island, NY, is an author, actor, and a theater director. He has worked as an actor in Japan, Germany, Australia, Ireland, and around the United States, and also worked as a fisherman for five seasons.

Along with his novels, *A Winsome Murder, The Silenced, Blue,* and *Indifferent Red* (Fall 2021), Jim has also worked extensively as a playwright. His adult plays for the stage include: *An Improbable Fiction, Christmas in Babylon, Learning to Stay, Gift of the Magi* (a musical adaptation); *In Acting Shakespeare; The Desert Queen* (the life of Gertrude Bell); *Dickens In America; Waiting for Vern,* and a new adaptation of *Cyrano de Bergerac.* His work for young audiences has been acknowledged with The Distinguished Play Award from The American Alliance of Theater and Education; The Intellectual Freedom Award by the Kentucky Council of Teachers of English/Language Arts; the Shubert Fendrich Memorial Playwriting Contest, and The American Alliance of Theater and Education honored his body of work with the Charlotte B. Chorpenning Award.

Jim is a recipient of the National Endowment for the Arts Literature Fellowship for Fiction, and a member of The Dramatists Guild and Actors Equity Association.

His education began as a first mate on the charter boat JIB VII out of Captree Boat Basin, NY, where he worked for five seasons. He then studied theater at Suffolk County Community College, Long Island, where he received an AS degree, and at the University of Wisconsin-Milwaukee, where he received a BFA. He also attended Madison Area Technical College where he was licensed as an Emergency Medical Technician. He lives in a small town in Wisconsin.

www.ingramcontent.com/pod-product-compliance
Ingram Content Group UK Ltd.
Pitfield, Milton Keynes, MK11 3LW, UK
UKHW021053270726
13967UKWH00012B/634

9 781736 651247